Top 100 Internet mistakes you can't afford to make

Top 100 Internet mistakes you can't afford to make

Peter Burns

THE McGRAW-HILL COMPANIES

London · Burr Ridge IL · New York · St Louis · San Francisco
Auckland · Bogotá · Caracas · Lisbon · Madrid · Medico · Milan
Montreal · New Delhi · Panama · Paris · San Juan · São Paulo
Singapore · Sydney · Tokyo · Toronto

Published by McGraw-Hill Professional
Shoppenhangers Road
Maidenhead
Berkshire
SL6 2QL
Telephone: 44 (0) 1628 502 500
Fax: 44 (0) 1628 770 224
Website: www.mcgraw-hill.co.uk

Sponsoring Editor: Elizabeth Robinson
Editorial Assistant: Sarah Wilks
Business Marketing Manager: Elizabeth McKeever
Senior Production Manager: Max Elvey

Produced for McGraw-Hill by Steven Gardiner Ltd
Text design by Steven Gardiner Ltd
Printed and bound in Great Britain by Bell & Bain Ltd, Glasgow
Cover design by Senate Design Ltd

McGraw-Hill

A Division of The **McGraw·Hill** Companies

British Library Cataloguing in Publication Data
A catalogue record for this book is available from the British Library

Library of Congress Cataloguing in Publication Data
The Library of Congress data for this book
has been applied for from the Library of Congress

ISBN 0 07 709879 X

McGraw-Hill books are available at special quantity discounts.
Please contact the Corporate Sales Executive at the above address.

This book is dedicated to Anna

Contents

Introduction

Now, more than ever before, Internet ventures are a risk. With any risk, you're bound to make mistakes. However, with the pressure to produce real returns on your investment, there's little room to make a mistake once, let alone twice.

This book is a straightforward guide to recognising and avoiding the 100 most common and potentially damaging Internet mistakes you can make. Each mistake is analysed in separate chapters that are quick to read and get straight to the ideas and pointers you can use to guide your own new-media projects. Each chapter covers:

- Details of the mistake and what to do to solve it. Only a basic knowledge of the Internet is assumed.
- Where you can get further information, including websites, other related mistakes and useful books. (To find any of the books, simply search on the title in any online bookstore.)
- Technical terms, which are marked in **bold** and explained in the glossary at the back of the book.

Starting with the most important, the mistakes are ranked from 1 to 100, but use this ranking only as a general guide, as their importance will depend on a wide range of individual factors. To use the book, read each mistake in order, or dip in to chapters for inspiration. Alternatively, the list is also classified into the three key areas of Internet business – Design, Marketing and Strategy. Whatever way you use it, you'll find this book provides you with an all-round guide to best Internet practice.

If you have any feedback or suggestions, please email me at:
peter@100mistakes.com

Peter Burns

The Top 100 Internet Mistakes

Page download time of over eight seconds

1

The mistake | Design   Marketing   Strategy

Download speed is users' top complaint about the Internet. The growth of web features and flash graphics in order to stand out from the crowd has raced well-ahead of the growth in connection speeds. As a result, users leave sites prematurely, whilst online retailers lose millions in revenue.

The best performing sites average page downloads of five seconds according to the weekly Keynote UK Internet Performance Index. Sites like Yahoo! regularly respond in less than one second, with worst performers reaching 15 seconds or more.

Despite promises of widespread **broadband** Internet access and high-speed connections at work, Forrester Research Inc estimated that in 2000, almost 80 per cent of UK users still used standard telephone-line connections to access the Internet. A landmark study in 1999 by Zona Research created the 'eight-second rule' before which users bailout of slow sites. Since then, users' impatience has grown steadily and has been adversely affected by the download speed of other new-media platforms, such as **WAP**.

As well as competitive pressures, the reason is that companies take an 'inside-out' approach to monitoring their Internet performance. You may have the latest **servers**, and websites may perform well in the boardroom, but this often masks the true performance on users' PCs.

The solution

An 'outside-in' approach is required. Download speed is a product of page size + transmission delays + processing time.

The first step is balancing page size and content. You have to design for the connection of your audience but a general site should design to the lowest connection. A page size below 50K is preferable, below 40K as with sites such as Yahoo.com and Lycos.com, is even better.

VERY IMPORTANT

You can't do anything about high traffic slowing down general Internet performance. However, if you use an external web host for your **servers** you should ensure that you agree prior performance levels and hold them accountable. The same applies if you use an advertising network (for serving your website-banner inventory). Can you rely on the speed of their servers to download your banner advertising?

VERY
IMPORTANT

Testing should also take an outside-in approach. Your agency or developers must test over a standard dial-up account to get the true user experience. Download can also be seriously affected by too much traffic, so load testing should be another regular development task, particularly before major events or seasonal demand surges. Monitoring your competitors' sites in the same way will also provide you with valuable benchmarks. Agencies such as Keynote can outsource this monitoring and reporting for you.

Minimising download is about developing for your users. As a first step, aim at reducing page download time by just one second, and you should achieve a significant improvement in both traffic and e-commerce revenue.

Further information

www.keynote.com
www.zonaresearch.com
Mistake 68 – Lack of load testing, see p. 136
Mistake 66 – Video streaming quality, see p. 132

3

2 Lack of funding

The mistake   Design   Marketing   **Strategy**

Obtaining investment for any UK business is difficult. Small online companies look to bank loans, although banks do not always give consideration to the problems faced in new media. Larger companies turn to private investment but, given the dramatic fall in stocks, funding for new or existing projects can be hard to find. As a result, many high-profile ventures such as dressmart.com and clickmango.com have closed due to a lack of second or third-round funding.

The recent downturn in the industry does not mean that investment has dried up, rather that investors are more cautious and selective. A company needs more than a unique idea and **domain** name – solid business plans and strong management are required to convince investors that a project will produce returns, whether the investor is the internal finance director, local bank manager or a venture capitalist.

The solution

VERY IMPORTANT

A succinct business plan is vital in sourcing funding, covering the usual elements of product, marketing and financial strategies. In an Internet business plan you have to be up front and realistic about the risks and build in key goals (financial, marketing, strategic partnerships, etc.) over the first few years.

VERY IMPORTANT

For loans, banks will look at a small Internet venture like any other business, although some, e.g. Lloyds TSB, have particular experience in e-commerce. Companies looking for a larger investment, generally over £100,000, should consider venture-capitalist firms that offer funds in return for an equity stake in the business. Venture capital is only viable if the business can show relatively rapid and sustained growth, as investors are unlikely to be interested if they cannot see a return within five years. Industry sector, geographical location, stage of development and 'fashion' affect response. For example, business-to-business enterprises were in favour in 2000/2001, along with wireless and industry-specific business portals. Investors look for a good rate of return and appropriate 'exit points' where they can cash in their investment, so indicating these in a plan will help. Offering investors a seat on the management board, and highlighting any existing assets the company already has, also helps to build their confidence. The best starting point for venture capital is the British Venture Capital Association (BVCA).

4

Companies that fall in-between the resources of banks and venture capitalists may be lucky enough to find a 'Business Angel', who invest smaller amounts in younger companies. Usually private individuals, they can be approached by intermediary 'introduction' networks such as firsttuesday.co.uk, findyourangel.com and www.nationalbusangels.co.uk.

New-media ventures are no longer just seen as Internet businesses but businesses in their own right. It is possible to find an investor but, unlike the rush to market of previous years, plans must be backed up with unique ideas, realistic financial projections and an experienced management team.

Further information

www.bvca.co.uk (guides to venture capital and business angels)
www.venturedome.co.uk (venture capital portal)
www.e-cradle.co.uk (useful resource and funding portal)
www.eisa.org.uk (offers tax relief to qualifying companies, making them more attractive to investors)

5

3 Lack of an eCRM strategy

Customer Relationship Management is a well used but often misunderstood process. eCRM allows companies to get closer to their customers through a combination of acquisition, relationship building via data management, as well as using it to facilitate e-commerce. Other than large scale businesses, few small- to medium-sized enterprises are implementing it effectively.

> Almost half of European businesses do not see CRM as 'critical' to their success. Almost a third have no interest at all in implementing CRM.
>
> *Source*: International Data Corporation, March 2001

There are a number of common errors when implementing eCRM: too much focus on technology; seeing eCRM as web or email communication only and assuming it allows every customer to be given the same personalised message. The result is overly expensive software which, in practice, still produces quite rudimentary solutions.

The solution

An eCRM solution is impossible to summarise succinctly but is best described in terms of the most common difficulties:

Focus on technology
Although it is easy to see the application of personalised rich-media emails or live text chat over the website, eCRM is as much about people as it is process. Software can capture data but needs human interpretation to be applied as useful information. Companies need to be cautious with the many CRM software vendors who will promise a whole range of costly technology. Simple scalable solutions work better than trying to implement everything at once.

Treating everyone the same

Some companies see all their customers as valuable and see eCRM as a method to create the same level of personalisation for everyone. But every company will have the usual 20 per cent of top-tier valuable customers. This is where eCRM development should be focused, especially as these customers will bring in the revenue to pay for what are often costly eCRM solutions. Customers should, therefore, be segmented in terms of their economic value to the company, as well as their behavioural value, such as buying habits or demographics.

Planning
Like any project it is important to plan. A study in 2000 by Gartner Group estimated that by 2004, only 35 per cent of companies will have defined their desired costs and benefits from eCRM before implementation.

Corporate culture
The most common reason for failure to implement eCRM is organisational resistance. This is because eCRM extends beyond a website to all areas of the company that interact with customers. Data and departments need to be integrated and this is best achieved with top-management support and a separate project leader with cross-department responsibility.

The principles of eCRM are the same as CRM. Companies should not give too much importance to the 'e' as it is just another channel in reaching consumers. And, unlike the rest of the Internet, there is no guarantee that eCRM will build loyalty any faster than CRM as they both deal with the same customer. CRM is a philosophy rather than technology and companies need to at least change their way of thinking if they are to get the most out of their online customer relationships.

Further information
www.ecrmguide.com (CRM news)
www.crm-forum.com (CRM portal)
Essential Guide to Knowledge Management (eCRM guide by Tiwana)
Mistake 4 – Lack of an email marketing plan, *see p. 8*
Mistake 28 – Mass personalisation, *see p. 56*
Mistake 47 – Lack of staff buy-in, *see p. 94*

4 Lack of an email marketing strategy

The mistake	Design	Marketing	**Strategy**

VERY
IMPORTANT

Email is a cost-effective and flexible method of communication that compares favourably with traditional direct mail. Email can produce double-digit response rates compared to the 3 per cent average for direct mail.

An increasing number of companies are using email, either with tactical, *ad hoc* campaigns or with a regular e-newsletter, which smaller companies tend to manage with basic home-grown solutions. With over 3 billion commercial email messages sent in 2001, if these communications are not managed correctly then the hard work in building the initial contacts can be quickly eroded.

It's not enough to collect customer email addresses, or just to send out a monthly email communication – companies need a structured plan in order to use addresses effectively.

The solution

Objectives
Before you start any campaign you need to be clear of your objectives and how you are going to measure response. Are you looking to drive site traffic, convert prospects to customers, educate or cross or up sell?

Collect names
There are a number of methods of creating an email address list. The simplest is any area where you collect customer information, be that over the phone or via the website. You need to be clear what the benefit of giving such personal data will be and get explicit permission to send marketing communications if you want to avoid sending **spam**. For this reason, buying into third party email lists is not recommended.

VERY
IMPORTANT

Format
You can choose from a wide range of email formats, such as text, **HTML** or rich media that include video or animated elements. The latter cost more and not everyone who has email can see rich media nor necessarily has Internet access. Above all, make sure the format doesn't take precedence over the actual message.

Personalisation

Seen to be the key to effective email campaigns, you can get greater response by offering different versions of your email based on customer information when they first register. More sophisticated software is needed if you wish to base email content on an analysis of individuals' site usage and purchase patterns.

Who sends it?

Smaller companies can purchase bulk email software packages, which are ideal for sending to lists of several thousand at a time. Larger organisations will find it more effective to outsource the process to companies such as Message Media or 24/7 Media.

Frequency

The most popular email frequency is monthly, but this tends to be chosen as a matter of course rather than by customer preference. It also means that you may have to send out emails when you really don't have much to say. Unless your customer offering changes regularly, planning for a set number of emails a year, but not specifying a regular date will have greater impact.

Measurement

Email campaign measurement should be compared against traditional direct mail but also has different elements. For example, how many respond to your email by clicking on links or sending a return email? How many unsubscribe, what is the speed of response and how many emails are undeliverable?

Email marketing should be a long-term commitment as opposed to a monthly chore carried out by the marketing team. Given the increasing volume of commercial email, high average response rates will fall, as happened with banners. Companies therefore need to invest in staff, software and a structured programme if they want it to be successful.

Further information

www.messagemedia.com
www.247europe.com
Email Marketing (useful book by Sterne)
Mistake 27 – Undeliverable email, see p. 54
Mistake 5 – Email response time over six hours, see p. 10
Mistake 51 – Careless email copy, see p. 102

5 Email response time over six hours

Email is an essential element of any website's customer service. Regular Internet users rank it higher than the phone or post. The proliferation of email has also created ever-rising expectations – whereas two years ago, a week would have been an acceptable response time, six hours is now considered the norm. Yet go to many a website and it's hard to even find contact details. And, when you do, you are unlikely to hear back within a week let alone six hours.

VERY IMPORTANT

Companies are improving their response times but it lags far behind the growth in email volumes. The problem lies in poor strategies to deal with incoming emails and low budgets. Poor response generates even more emails from users and eventually site abandonment, making a mockery of the huge sums often spent on marketing to generate site traffic in the first place.

VERY IMPORTANT

The solution

Choose between quick fixes and long-term solutions:

Quick fix

- Make your contact details easy to find on your site.
- Encourage users to contact you by other means, especially if they have more internal resource – phone, fax or post.
- Monitor the most frequently asked email questions and answer them on your site, to minimise enquiries.
- Auto-acknowledge emails – the majority of sites still don't. By doing so, customers will wait longer before sending follow-up emails, buying you some valuable response time.
- Use your site statistics to monitor user paths through sites and at what point they send emails – a simple way to indicate service bottlenecks.

Longer term

Once you have sorted the quick fixes, you need to examine both email prioritisation and auto reply. Prioritisation allows you to devote more resource to your most valuable customers. You can identify emails for priority response if they are from existing customers on your database or are generated from key areas of your site (such as online sales).

Auto reply is more than auto acknowledgement. It involves software to pick out key phrases in the email and select appropriate responses. Most managers' distrust of this non-human intervention soon subsides when they see the high levels of accuracy, often over 90 per cent. A step towards this is auto-suggest software, whereby the automated reply is sent to customer-service staff for a quick check before it is sent. Any company can apply these principles but, for larger organisations, you will need to invest in specialists for this type of software, such as Siebel or Oracle.

Further information

www.oracle.com
www.siebel.com
Mistake 32 – Lack of call-centre integration, see p. 64

6 Poor navigation

Navigation is the user's aid to completing a task, whether that is gathering information or making an online purchase. Although it is one of the key determinants of usability, poor navigation continues to account for high levels of website abandonment.

(handwritten margin note: ★★ OK — VERY IMPORTANT)

> 49 per cent of users report being unsatisfied by the levels of intuitive navigation on the Internet
>
> *Source*: Mondalis Research Technologies, 2001

It occurs when design is seen as more important than the user experience. Users' biggest issue is not knowing the context of the page they are in and how to move forward or back, particularly if they enter a page direct (e.g. via a search engine), rather than via a home page. Difficulties arise with text or visual icons that are not intuitive, or the lack of a clear difference between content and navigation. There is also dissatisfaction with the majority of search functions, a key navigational tool.

However, the importance of structure has given rise to over-navigation, and too many choices can overwhelm users. You can see this development in many US airline sites, where you can access almost everything from the home page and the site starts to look like a portal.

(handwritten margin note: VERY IMPORTANT)

The solution

There is no one right way to design navigation but look at your site and consider the following points:

Intuition
Usability success is a result of creating intuitive and obvious structure. This is where usability testing is important, especially as your navigation must be efficient in dealing with different levels of user expertise.

Context
Look at any page of your site and ask yourself whether users can answer three questions: where am I, where can I go next, and how do I get back? Key

(handwritten margin note: VERY IMPORTANT)

information such as search or contacts should be accessible on every page in the same place.

Navigation tools

You must invest in your search function – like a shop assistant, your search function should provide instant answers to users' queries. Site maps need to be comprehensive and simple, as they tend to be users' last attempt to find what they need. You can also develop visual, 3D or even virtual-reality site maps but, until faster **broadband** connections dominate, are best avoided. Rollovers, that highlight as your mouse passes over them are also useful; some studies have shown them to increase usability by up to 30 per cent.

VERY IMPORTANT

Be direct

There's a temptation to use smart or witty labels in your navigation and links, or elaborately designed icons. Navigation has to be clear and direct – it might look boring to your designers or marketers, but it won't be for your users.

VERY IMPORTANT

Innovation isn't necessarily good

Users learn web navigation by repetition. So your site should keep the principles used by the majority of other sites, rather than trying to reinvent them.

Above all, ensure your navigation is consistent and intuitive – it could be the key to your competitive differentiation.

Further information

Web Works Navigation (book of case studies by Couplan)
Mistake 16 – Ineffective search, see p. 32
Mistake 37 – Information-poor homepage, see p. 74
Mistake 81 – Long scrolling pages, see p. 162

7 Not measuring website ROI

The mistake

In 1999 and 2000, businesses were most interested in being first to market with Internet ventures, seeing lost time as lost revenue. As hundreds of European dot com companies have discovered, this approach may have been short-sighted. Securing funds for Internet ventures, from the bank or finance director, now requires greater accountability

> 77 per cent of IT and ebusiness executives said they would increase their Internet spending in 2001. However, these ebusiness projects are under increasing pressure to show profits.
>
> *Source: Internet Week,* January 2001

However, those who do measure return on investment (ROI) are doing it unrealistically or on a small scale. They have poor technology to mine data from existing ventures, rely on traditional metrics such as website hits or database volumes, or the job is seen as one for webmasters rather than core to management decision-making.

The solution

Measuring ROI depends on business goals and can be complicated. However, you must bear in mind the following:

Customer return
Growth in site traffic of 200 per cent or widespread PR may look impressive but consider how it improves the customer-buying process and, in particular, targets valuable customer segments or improves customer service.

Cross-company return
A website impacts on an entire organisation and ROI metrics should reflect this. For example, call-centre processes will change, human resources will process job applications online and marketing will have more cost-effective advertising tools. This should be measured continuously, not just when a project is first designed.

VERY IMPORTANT

Metrics

There are many, but consider metrics from site-traffic, sales, customer demographics and marketing activity. Other metrics include time to market, time for the competition to copy you, loyalty and repeat purchases, back-end reliability and **hosting**. Above all ROI metrics must be simple, quantifiable and meaningful, which generally means how they affect profitability.

Real-time return

Is the key to ROI measurement, allowing for instant optimisation to improve effectiveness. Already used with online advertising, improved software packages are making it more widely available.

Staff training

Training in how to measure ROI is rarely given but sorely needed. Gartner Group estimate that by 2005, companies will need three times more staff working on analytics as are needed today.

VERY IMPORTANT

Measuring ROI is an evolving process that can never be 100 per cent accurate but is increasingly essential. Otherwise you may find that the premise 'we can't afford not to be online' is actually untrue.

Further information

www.computerworld.com/roi (helpful ROI magazine)

Mistake 62 – Not auditing your website, see p. 124
Mistake 52 – Not analysing site statistics, see p. 104

8 Limited user feedback

The mistake	Design	Marketing Strategy

Whereas traditional customer feedback meant a written letter or occasional focus-group research, the Internet has created much faster and more personal feedback channels.

The ease at which customers can feedback online creates resource problems in dealing with the volume, so even basic email contacts become either non-existent or buried in a website – for example UK insurance provider Tesco Finance lacked an online feedback mechanism on its site in 2001. There are now a growing number of third-party feedback sites such as planetfeedback.com or dooyoo.co.uk and, in extreme cases, customers will vent their anger by setting up their own anti-corporate website.

Companies can no longer ignore or pay lip service to online feedback – they must encourage it. If they don't, customers will simply do it elsewhere.

The solution

Survey

Online surveys increase the speed at which you can gather customer opinion. There are a number of software packages that can do the analysis for you such as WebSurveyor. Alternatively, you can employ dedicated agencies such as Confirmit who will manage the process for you.

Process points

Building feedback mechanisms into the buying process can generate higher responses. A pre-sale survey can ask what consumers want, whereas a simple after-sale email can ask what they think of their purchase. Overall, it gives customers the feeling that they are a part of the product-development process and will generate a higher response than random surveys that **pop-up** across your site.

Peer-to-peer

Peer-to-peer feedback encourages customers to review or rate products for the benefit of other customers. Used successfully by the likes of WHSmith.co.uk they encourage trust in the site although need to be constantly monitored.

Consumer clubs

Some products have migrated their telephone carelines into online forums as a way to gather feedback. Dolmio (dolmio.com), the cooking sauce manufactured by Mars, adopted this approach, using their website solely as a feedback mechanism.

Reward

Feedback response can be higher if you offer a reward, but this should be product-related (such as discounts) to discourage competition entrants. It can be of greater value if it is targeted at a closed user group, such as an after-sales email list.

Site statistics

Website statistics can give general clues to customer opinion, simply by looking at the most popular pages, the paths which customers take through the site or the points at which they exit.

Some businesses are better suited to certain feedback channels (e.g. peer-to-peer) but all can benefit from encouraging it. Online feedback is also more honest as it is seen to be anonymous. In return, promoting feedback channels helps to engender trust (a quality sorely missing in e-business transactions), spot trends, cross sell and, most importantly, allow your site and products to evolve.

Further information

www.websurveyor.com
www.confirmit.com
Mistake 54 – Anti-corporate websites, see p. 108
Mistake 53 – Lack of community, see p. 106

17

9 Lack of trust

The mistake   Design   Marketing   **Strategy**

Given the Internet's relative infancy compared to other media, consumers have always had problems trusting online companies. Low barriers to entry have produced many a new Internet start-up – trying to build an instant brand, over promising and under-delivering. The closure of many high-profile companies such as cdnow.co.uk and etoys.com, has made the problem worse.

Almost two-thirds of online consumers are unlikely to trust an e-commerce website. This is because of an inability to meet expectations, particularly in the areas of security and customer service, meaning that companies need to work hard at building trust. When Siemens and British Telecom commissioned a report on trust, it showed that bbc.co.uk is the UK's most trusted site, and websites from major established retailers such as Marks and Spencer and W. H. Smith are now considered trustworthier than Amazon. Internet-only brands therefore need to work the hardest, as established brands begin to translate the trust they have developed offline over time, to their online services.

The solution

Trust develops from every area of a business that impacts on the customer experience. Consider the following:

Exposure
Trust comes from familiarity over time. Regular and consistent interaction with customers will therefore do more for trust than spending large sums on advertising. Sites with strong backing make it clear they are supported by established brands, such as Egg.com backed by the Prudential – thereby exposing the site to the trust associated with the backer.

Security
One of the key elements in building trust. Users need to know you are using the latest technology to secure their personal and financial data. Recognised security schemes, such as BT TrustWise, Verisign or Microsoft Passport create assurances, as do third-party codes of conduct or 'seals of approval' such as Which Web Trader.

18

Human elements

Particularly important in retail, consumers trust information if it is communicated face to face. So, offer clear contact information online, and integration with your call centre or offline stores. Testimonials from other customers can also be useful.

IMPORTANT Localise

Users prefer and trust local and personalised content that is relevant to them.

Be upfront

Honesty builds trust in any relationship. Be clear about how personal information is used with a privacy policy, don't hide stock availability, delivery or pricing information and, where possible, offer customer service or fraud guarantees.

Sensitive communications

When a customer opts into your database, that isn't a sign to bombard them with every update to your site. Use email communications sparsely and your consumers will give messages greater value.

Damage limitation

Trust is easily damaged when things go wrong. Email is now the preferred channel for customer complaints so deal with them quickly.

Further information

www.verisign.com
www.which.net/webtrader
Mistake 48 – Creating unattainable expectations, see p. 96
Mistake 29 – Lack of a human face, see p. 58
Mistake 21 – Unsecure servers, see p. 42

10 Spam

Design **Marketing** Strategy

The mistake

Spam is the sending of indiscriminate, unsolicited commercial email. It represents an estimated €10bn a year in wasted connection charges alone, which equates to 10–15 per cent of all email communications.

Whereas spam has traditionally been associated with unknown brands and false or misleading offers, reputable companies need to be careful. If recipients even think you are sending spam, they can easily block out addresses using filtering software, built into many email packages. There's a fine line between effective commercial email and spam and companies need to avoid the negative impact and tarnished reputation associated with it.

The solution

The simple answer is to follow the principles of 'permission marketing' – users must opt-in to all communication sent to them. This is contrary to many data-capture practices (e.g. with registration forms) where users have to 'opt out' of future communications from the company but have to 'opt in' to communications from 'reputable third parties'. Marketers are concerned that 'opt-in' will drastically reduce the size of their databases, but just because someone opts out from your email doesn't necessarily mean they don't want other forms of communication.

Buying bulk email addresses from list brokers is not the same as with direct mail. Email is a lot more intrusive and such bulk buying or using email to prospect for new clients is best avoided. You also need to distance your emails from the practices used by spammers. Therefore your email must have genuine value. If you have the database capabilities to produce personalised emails, this doesn't necessarily mean you should use a personal tone. Also ensure there is an email return address that recipients can reply to, whatever their query.

You should never try and hide the fact that your email is commercial, nor hide privacy policies or unsubscribe processes. In particular, if your privacy policy does change significantly, you should explicitly tell your users, rather than make subtle changes to the policy, which most people never read in full anyway. There are also third-party schemes such as the Direct Marketing Association's e-Mail Preference Service, which brings customers and companies together. This builds trust in the participating companies who agree to stringent communication policies.

Just as was the case with junk direct mail and junk faxes, legislation will be a key solution to the problem. Already countries such as Denmark, Germany and Italy require explicit 'opt-in' clauses in email communication. This is also being proposed by the European Commission.

Spam by definition is indiscriminate and can be avoided with better targeting. Although reputable companies don't send spam in the traditional sense, the real issue is user perception of spam. A few simple mistakes can be enough to destroy expectations and any chance of a long-term customer relationship.

Further information

www.dma.org.uk (Direct Marketing Association)
www.cauce.org (Coalition Against Unsolicited Commercial Email)
Mistake 86 – Wireless spam, see p. 172
Mistake 13 – Ignoring the Data Protection Act, see p. 26

Lack of a search-engine strategy

The mistake   Design   Marketing   **Strategy**

From a marketing perspective, search engines aren't as useful as they used to be. Back in 1998, they only referenced a third of the web – in 2001 this dropped to less than 10 per cent.

Nonetheless, over two-thirds of web users rely on search engines and it's the first port of call for new users. The key search engines – Yahoo, Excite, Altavista and Lycos have all become content-rich news, sport and entertainment destinations in their own right. Yet most major brands still don't have a search-engine strategy, although they might have registered the site when it first launched.

Even if a site is maintained by an agency, they will either not have the expertise and/or will charge dearly for it. A poor strategy both loses potential traffic and can have negative brand implications if you do not rank highly.

You cannot rely solely on search engines to boost traffic, however, it's a cost-effective solution that must form part of every marketing plan.

The solution

There are two solutions. Do it yourself, or use one of a growing number of search-engine 'specialists'. The DIY option is ideal on a low budget. Software, such as Web Position Gold and Top Dog, priced at around £100, can index your site automatically with specific keywords or phrases you provide – with reasonable results showing after two or three months.

The specialist companies, such as NetBooster or WebGravity, all have slightly different approaches. However, their main weapons will be one of two choices:

- Organising all the submissions for you which will include keyword selection and advice on site design to maximise ranking. Plus regular reviews, competitor comparisons and, importantly, re-submissions.
- Creating 'gateway' pages for key areas of your site – these are specially designed to rank highly in search engines and then link to your main site – smart, but not if your site has dynamic content as gateway pages are static.

Expect to pay £1000–£1500 per page, submitted on an annual contract. Many of these specialists offer some guarantee of results, so this could be money well spent.

The final option is to play the specialists at their own game and learn the full rules of search-engine submission – but only choose this option if you've time on your hands. Understanding the submission process is a job in itself.

Further information

www.webposition.com
www.netbooster.co.uk
www.topdog.com
www.webgravity.co.uk
Search Engine Positioning (useful book by Marckini)
Mistake 88 – Not paying for search-engine listings, see p. 176

12 Lack of usability evaluation

Usability, or the development of clear, intuitive web interfaces is still a challenge to most companies. They must balance increasing content volume, new forms of advertising and new applications to remain competitive. Shorter deadlines mean that companies are making too many assumptions about what users want – or what they think they want. The result is a poor user experience:

- poorly labelled and slow links
- out-of-date and difficult to find content
- advertising that looks like content
- search functions that are too broad.

VERY IMPORTANT

Companies do look for user evaluation but usually after the site has been designed. It's a lot more costly to make changes later, rather than getting users involved from the outset.

The solution

There are a number of ways you can involve users in the evaluation of your web interface:

Usability consultants
Most major management consultancies, such as Accenture, have experts in usability. They organise and interpret evaluation, although their services won't come cheap.

Focus groups
The best advice is from users themselves. You don't have to hire expensive research rooms. Get them into your office or hire out the local Internet café for a few hours one evening. Plus, use regular registered users as well as people who have never been to your site, for different perspectives.

Log files
All site-statistics packages, such as WebTrends, have data on common paths users have taken through your site. Use this to determine where and where not your users are browsing.

Testing software

You'll find software that can automatically report on some of the more repetitive evaluation – be that listing broken links, unlabelled pages, or pages that are too slow to download. The best by far is Watchfire's Enterprise Solution, which automatically simulates and reports on user interactions or 'scenario testing' – such as product purchases.

Competitors

Finally, make sure that in all your reviews, you check out the competition – learn not only from them but, as importantly, what your users think of them?

Further information

www.useit.com (the website of usability consultant Jakob Nielson)
www.webtrends.co.uk
www.accenture.com
www.watchfire.com
Mistake 8 – Limited user feedback, *see p. 16*

13 Ignoring the Data Protection Act

There is much confusion around the Data Protection Act. Companies know of its existence but there is a lack of awareness of how it should be implemented. This is especially the case with Internet companies, where volume rather than processing of customer data has been seen as a measure of success.

> European companies are failing to comply with the Data Protection Act. The worst offenders are financial service providers, followed closely by retailers, utilities and telecomms companies.
>
> *Source*: Mondex International, March 2001

The majority of companies are not complying with the Act or do not have budgets with which to do so. Confusion generally occurs in three areas: opt-out clauses, using data outside of the European Union and new technologies such as **SMS** messaging.

Non-compliance can be a serious matter. Not only can it generate negative PR, the UK's Information Commissioner also has the right to demand evidence from companies and enforce notices or, ultimately, imprisonment.

The solution

Internet enterprises need to see themselves as direct-marketing operations, as much as is the case with traditional companies. All staff need to understand its importance particularly in the following areas:

Internal audit
Understand your current data-collection processes and how they can be improved.

Register
With the Data Protection Registrar if you have not already done so and nominate an employee with overall data-protection responsibility.

Third parties
To whom you outsource operations must also comply with the Act.

Moving data

To countries outside the European Union is only allowed if customers are notified and the countries can ensure adequate protection of the data. Amazon.co.uk was accused of violating the Act in September 2000 after they passed UK customer-data to their US office.

Get consent

From customers in order to use their data, using online 'opt-out' or preferably 'opt-in' boxes. Be clear how their data will be used, especially if it is sensitive, in areas such as race or religion.

Privacy policies

Need to be online and customers should be notified of them. A policy also needs to be actioned, not just something you add to your site in order to comply. If your site uses **cookies**, this should also be made clear.

Keep records up to date

Particularly from customers who unsubscribe from your services.

New technology

There is confusion about how the Act (and the associated Telecommunications Directive) applies to email, mobile and SMS messaging. If in any doubt, the 'gain customers' consent' rule should apply.

Already the importance of data protection is being updated with the European Electronic Communications Privacy Directive. In the meantime companies must be aware of the pitfalls. They can not only alienate customers but also have severe legal consequences.

Further information

www.dataprotection.gov.uk
www.dma.org.uk (Direct Marketing Association)
www.wirelessmarketing.org.uk (Wireless Marketing Association)
Mistake 97 – Hiding user policies, see p. 194
Mistake 86 – Wireless spam, see p. 172
Mistake 38 – Cookie mismanagement, see p. 76
Mistake 10 – Spam, see p. 20

14 No online-payment system

With European e-commerce expected to top $1 trillion by 2004, you would think that the majority of retailers would accept online transactions. Whereas large companies have the resource to invest in online-payment systems, a survey by Continental Research in 2000 showed that over 80 per cent of UK small businesses have never sold anything over the Internet.

Ignoring the value of online sales is often a consequence of a company not having, or being unable to get, a merchant account with a bank (especially if it is a start-up). Companies are also discouraged by fears of fraud and insufficient revenues.

The reality is that for smaller companies, there has never been a more cost-effective time to turn your website into an e-commerce operation.

The solution

The most widespread online payment is Visa credit card. Companies without merchant accounts from their bank should consider the services of a payment service provider (PSP), such as WorldPay or Datacash. They will offer you a package that you can add to your existing site to create a seamless user experience (e-commerce software now comes pre-set for working with some of the major PSPs). When choosing a PSP you need to ask a number of questions, as they all offer similar products:

- What are your set up and monthly/annual charges?
- What are the fees for each transaction (can be 4–8 per cent or higher for debit cards)?
- What cards and currencies can you support? Plus can you support VAT for European transactions?
- How many simultaneous user transactions can you guarantee at any one time?
- Do you offer free 24-hour support?
- Are your packages scalable?

If you are already trading with a merchant account, you can use a low-cost secure email system (such as that offered by Barclays.com), to transfer credit-card data. But the transaction is still processed offline, which customers can find irritating, so it is preferable to upgrade to a live process. Some of the main high-street banks have caught on to the value of offering packaged e-merchant accounts, but you will need a strong business plan to secure an account.

Online fraud, despite being ten times more likely than in offline stores, can be minimised by your choice of PSP. Minimise the risk by ensuring your PSP uses reputable online credit-reference agencies such as Experian, which claims it can spot over 95 per cent of online credit-card fraud. Some PSPs such as WorldPay also offer online fraud guarantees. Testing is also vital, even with software from the main banks, as your reputation cannot afford glitches concerning customers' credit cards.

Credit-card usage online dominates, partly due to a lack of alternatives. However, you may also consider cashless options in addition to, rather than instead of, credit-card payment systems. Online bank Egg.com, for example, has e-wallets, which you top up with credit and then use to shop online. Paybox also offers products that allow you to charge purchases to customers' mobile phone bills. E-loyalty points or incentives can also supplement your main payment system.

Packaged solutions offer you cost-effective online payment systems and implementation can take a matter of days. This can give websites, in particular, small- to medium-sized businesses, an instant lead over competitors with offline or poorly integrated payment systems.

Further information

www.worldpay.com
www.datacash.com
www.paybox.net
www.experian.com
Mistake 82 – Credit-card chargebacks, *p. 164*

15 Intrusive online advertising

Many websites rely on advertising for part or all of their revenue, but the majority of users find it annoying. The reality is that many users prefer accessing content for free with advertising, rather than the alternative of paying for it – yet advertising still causes irritation.

VERY IMPORTANT

> Over half of Internet users find online advertising irritating, over a fifth find it time-wasting and just under a fifth find it intrusive
>
> *Source*: Forrester Research Inc. User Monitor, 2000

Rich-media adverts such as **pop-ups** and **superstitials** cause more irritation than banners, as they interrupt both content and navigation. British Airways was the first UK company to use superstitials in 2000. Although it reported very high rates of click-through (up to 23 per cent) there was no report of the irritation experienced by those users that didn't respond.

Website owners are making the mistake of accepting all forms of rich-media adverts and not targeting them by user, time or site content. If advertising is the only revenue stream this may be forgivable, but is not a way to gain long-term user loyalty. Page design which makes content and advertising difficult to distinguish is another common error. This is important as users who see irritating adverts, will equally blame the media owner as well as the advertised brand.

The solution

Producing rich-media adverts can cost two or three times more than standard banners and the media-buying costs can be 50 per cent higher. Advertisers therefore need to work hard at being creative, encouraging engagement, interaction and optimised files, to minimise download speed.

VERY IMPORTANT

It is essential that rich-media adverts are well-targeted rather than run arbitrarily across a site. They should also be frequency capped. Although you will get diminishing click-throughs as a user sees an advert for the second and third time, the irritation level for other users increases. Media owners should have a policy for rich-media advertising, indicating frequency caps and pages that cannot run pop-up adverts (such as the home page or e-commerce shopping carts). More intrusive advertising also calls for monitoring of responses during the campaign and, if possible, adjusting as necessary to improve targeting, click-through and to minimise irritation. The Internet Advertising Bureau (IAB) is also developing several new forms of standard online adverts, so advertisers will not need to rely so much on rich-media solutions.

Advertisers like rich-media advertising given higher **click-through rates**. But they need to avoid poor use of the technology and poor targeting – the consequences of getting it wrong are much greater than using less intrusive methods.

Further information

www.iabuk.net (latest news from the IAB)
Mistake 65 – Over-use of banners, see p. 130

16 Ineffective search

Search is one of the key functions of website navigation and usability. Search tools are particularly important for content-rich information and retail sites with large product volumes – and are essential on sites with one hundred pages or more.

VERY
IMPORTANT

> 77 per cent of US online shoppers use a search function to find products and 43 per cent believe search functionality is the most important feature of online shopping.
>
> *Source:* PriceWaterhouse Coopers, March 2001

Many companies are not making the most of their online search, resulting in tools that are difficult to use and that produce slow and irrelevant results. There's also the tendency to add 'advanced search' options, when the basic function still needs improvement.

VERY
IMPORTANT

By investing in an effective search tool, you could be giving your users all the navigation they need.

The solution

Effective search should be both easy to use and accurate.

Easy to use
- Your search tool should be accessible from every page, ideally in the same position near the top.
- Users should be prompted as to which keywords to use – e.g. a list of the most popular keywords entered by other users or based on popular requests in your offline store.
- Avoid the tendency to bolt on external search-engine tools, unless absolutely necessary. They detract from your own search tool whilst encouraging users to leave your site.
- Some users prefer clicking on links, so include an up-to-date site content list and link to this from your search tool.
- If you do offer 'advanced search' with more options, make it less prominent than your basic search – e.g. as an additional refinement to the basic search.
- Don't leave users guessing on when they will see their search results. Give them an indication with an 'in progress' bar.

VERY
IMPORTANT

Accurate

Aim for quality not quantity. Don't list pages and pages of 'relevant' results as users will never look at them all. Given users' difficulty with keyword selection, results should be intelligent, offering alternative results for near match or mis-spelt keywords or for specific areas of your site.

Results also make more sense if they state where they fit within your site's overall navigation. Date and time is another useful addition.

Above all, the best way to understand how users search your site is to monitor them. Site statistics, search results and studies/books of how general search engines are used, will further help you to ensure your own search tool produces what your users are actually looking for.

Further information

www.nngroup.com/reports/ecommerce (29 design guidelines for better search from the Nielson Norman Group)

Web Developer.com Guide to Search Engines (useful book by Sonnereich and Macinta)

Mistake 6 – Poor navigation, see p. 12

17 Broken links

Design   Marketing   Strategy

The mistake

Despite being an age-old problem, broken links or '404 errors' are still prevalent on the Internet. It is estimated that broken links affect 10 per cent of all links on the Internet and are users' second greatest complaint behind speed. Yet the ability to link lies in the fundamentals of the web's rapid expansion.

VERY
IMPORTANT

Broken links reduce the credibility of a site and are the equivalent of contacting a call centre and then being abruptly cut off. Just as annoying but more difficult to track are links that are not broken, but direct to wrong or inappropriate pages.

Broken links apply to internal site links, external links to different sites and incoming links from other sites, including search-engine referrals. Despite readily available software, companies often lack a formal procedure to deal with or report broken links, especially if their site has constantly updated dynamic content.

The solution

Validation software
There are a number of link-validation software packages that can periodically check your site for broken internal and external links. Web-based solutions, such as Link Alarm, can automatically email the results to you. For larger sites, commercial software, such as Watchfire's LinkBot or Linkguard, will be more appropriate and have free or trial versions you can use. Larger corporate sites will find installing validation software direct to the site's server more effective. Perhaps the best validation of all is your users, often the first to feedback when they find a broken link.

Archive or redirect
There's an argument that all web pages should be kept online forever – this would prevent broken links. Although this makes sense if your site content lends itself to an archive, other pages have to be switched off (e.g. with out-of-date content or branding). In this case redirect the old page address to a new and relevant page, so incoming users don't get confronted with an error message.

Clearly written error messages
Minimise the annoyance if an incoming user does experience a broken link on your site, by copywriting all your error messages. Make sure there is also a form or email address so users can report the details of the error to you. Some companies, like Levi Strauss, have taken advantage of 404 messages by actually buying and adapting them for online advertisements.

Incoming links
In addition to the above points, try and monitor who is linking to your site to ensure their links are accurate – search-engines Hotbot and AltaVista have tools that can help monitor incoming links.

Above all, minimising broken links means taking the problem seriously, and creating a formal and regular internal validation procedure, especially as some links (such as those that are wrong but not broken) will not be picked out by automated software.

Further information
www.watchfire.com
www.linkguard.com
www.linkalarm.com
www.hotbot.co.uk (use advanced-search option)
www.altavista.com (type 'link:' followed by your web address to see who is linking to you)
Mistake 93 – Confusing error messages, see p. 186

18 Not maximising strategic links

Linking has been the basis of the Internet's rapid expansion and the success of many portals such as Yahoo! For years the basis of using links for marketing was barter by reciprocal linking. This strategy still applies today but has become a little more sophisticated.

Companies often see advertising as online banner, **pop-up** or email campaigns and linking as a useful tool for incremental traffic. Rich-media advertising, for example, is creative and seen as more interesting. Yet, select the right partner with high traffic levels or the right user demographics, and a simple text link can produce **click-through-rates** that far exceed those of banner advertising.

The solution

If you want successful links in the current market you will, in most cases, have to pay for them in one way or another:

Search engines

Regularly re-submitting your site to the major search engines will cost. The process is a job in itself so you will either have to devote one person's time to it or pay to outsource the process to a specialist company. Search engines such as Espotting.com or Overture.com (formerly GoTo.com) also accept links but rankings are based on how much each site is prepared to pay to be listed.

Traffic

High-traffic sites realise their position and will charge you for links. This is especially the case for portals that see links as advertising rather than providing an information service to users.

Retail

If your site's revenue is based on e-commerce then an affiliate programme is a useful way to increase both traffic and sales. Pioneered by Amazon, sites link to your site but are paid a commission in return if it results in a sale.

Content

VERY IMPORTANT

If your site is information-based then you can use your content as a bargaining tool for links. The news site, Guardian Unlimited, has made excellent use of this approach by allowing tens of thousands of web designers to automatically download headline feeds. The sites get live content and Guardian gets branding and **page impressions** in return, if anyone clicks on the headline. Content providers to Yahoo.co.uk's news service also provide their stories in return for links. Yet, in this case, the whole story (not just the headline) resides on Yahoo, given that their high-traffic levels give them greater bargaining power.

Choosing the right partner to link with is essential. This can often be seen with high-profile strategic alliances announced between major Internet brands – often the basis of them is a simple link to each others' sites. Checking who is currently linking to your site, using automated searches such as Link Popularity or Hotbot's Page Link Analyser, is a good starting point to look for partners. Links also need to be managed. Although one good strategic link will do more than hundreds of smaller reciprocal deals, they must all be monitored. Software such as Link Manager can be useful.

Links are still a powerful marketing tool, yet more and more you need to see them as advertising if you want to achieve significant results.

Further information

www.linkpopularity.com
www.linkmanager.com
www.hotbot.co.uk (select 'advanced search option')
Mistake 49 – Choosing the wrong web partner, see p. 98
Mistake 11 – Lack of a search-engine strategy, see p. 22
Mistake 88 – Not paying for search-engine listings, see p. 176

19 Abandoned shopping carts

Despite reports of the explosive growth in online shopping, it is estimated that up to 75 per cent of online shoppers still abandon their shopping carts before reaching the checkout. Industry experts estimate that 50 per cent of all revenue lost on e-tail sites is during the checkout process.

VERY IMPORTANT

> 55 per cent of abandoned carts occur prior to final checkout, whilst 32 per cent occur at the checkout when entering billing or shipping information, or after the final sale calculation.
>
> *Source*: BizRate.com Oct 2000, US survey

Customers get frustrated for a number of reasons:

- Difficult to find product and delivery information
- Slow loading pages
- Long or complicated registration forms
- Assumption that price is the main reason for shopping online
- Worries about online security
- Virtual shopping assistants that do more for company PR than the user experience.

VERY IMPORTANT

The high abandonment rate is due to a lack of understanding of why customers shop online and a preference for technology over user experience.

The solution

Navigation

This underlines the entire structure of your site. Finding product information must be easy. Virtual shop assistants are an option but are an expensive investment, and your money could be better spent creating an effective search tool.

Reduce download speed

Slow loading pages cause up to 50 per cent of abandoned carts according to Zona Research, with many e-tail pages taking twenty times longer to load in 2001 compared to 2000.

Non-buying activities

This should be essential if you sell offline, as online shoppers mainly use the Internet for research and price comparison. Car dealers such as Land Rover use this approach, to book free test drives via the website, which then gets customers into the showrooms.

Be upfront

VERY IMPORTANT

About product availability and delivery times and charges. Research has shown that up to two-thirds of online stores have failed to show product availability before users submit payment details.

Understand your customers

Your shopping process will need to reflect your customer base. For low-value items, for example, convenience ranks higher than price. Customers don't want to fill out long registration forms in order to buy, and so need security and delivery assurances.

Damage repair

There is much you can do to convert abandoned shoppers. Monitor your site statistics to see at which pages users abandon their carts. Capturing data at the page of abandonment can also be used to email users to encourage them (e.g. with offers) to return to the store to complete the purchase.

Customers do return to buy products abandoned online, but failing to improve checkout process means any future purchase will either be offline or with the nearest competitor.

Further information

www.actinic.co.uk (shopping-cart provider with useful reference information)

Mistake 70 – Not reacting to site abandonment, see p. 140
Mistake 55 – Poor product information, see p. 110
Mistake 29 – Lack of a human face, see p. 58

20 Domain mismanagement

A domain name is a company's web address and usually represents both brand and trademarks. The low cost of purchasing a domain name makes it easy to register variations on any name. Too many companies are finding that slow response to domain registration or ignorance of new domains results in long, costly legal battles.

> 90 per cent of companies have experienced some form of domain-name infringement.
>
> *Source*: Net Searcher Net Protection Survey, 2000

Companies regularly fail to register more than just the top-level domains (e.g. .com or .co.uk). If a problem arises, heavy-handed approaches are used which can create negative PR. Warner Brothers received press criticism when it approached fan sites using variations of their movie of the Harry Potter books, requesting the domains to be transferred to Warner Bros. EasyGroup, the holding company for sites such as the airline easyjet.com, has also been criticised for trying to reclaim many variations of easy.com. As a result, companies must carefully manage their domain portfolio, both before and after any potential dispute.

The solution

Portfolio management

This requires an audit to ensure all company and brand domains are purchased. It should include variations such as hyphenated spellings or mis-spellings. International domains should also be considered, especially for future expansion. Unless you have the resources of the BBC (which spent an estimated £500,000 in early 2001, registering 3000 new domain names), you will have to draw a line over how many you buy. Some newer domains, such as .tv, cost thousands of pounds a year to maintain. The work can also be outsourced to a number of domain name management agencies.

Renewals

It is estimated that up to a third of domain payments are neither paid nor renewed each year. If a company has many domains, the expiry dates should be carefully checked and renewed for long periods, five or ten years at a time.

Plan ahead

Many companies have announced new products and failed to register their web addresses in advance. Immediately after Warner Brothers announced their new Harry Potter movie, a cyber-squatter bought over 100 variations of the name, which Warner Brothers had to claim back. When British Telecom announced two major divisions, 'BT Wireless' and 'Future BT', they failed to register variations of the name, which were quickly taken by other individuals.

Resolution

If a company lays claim to a domain they must be clear that they have the rights. Cyber-squatting cases normally fall in favour of the company, for example, when a squatter threatened to sell children's-bbc.co.uk to an adult site if the BBC did not buy it. Conversely, the BBC had to pay an estimated £200,000 to US firm Boston Business Computing who legitimately owned bbc.com. Before going to court, companies should consider the mediation services of domain registrar Nominet (which covers domains ending in .uk) or ICANN (which covers .com, .org and .net domains).

Protecting company and brand names shouldn't be done in court. Avoid the cost with domain awareness and a structured domain-management programme.

Further information

www.nic.uk (Nominet)
www.icann.org (Internet Corporation for Assigned Names & Numbers)
www.domainnotes.com (useful reference site)
www.unclaimeddomains.com (list of recently unpaid domain renewals)
Mistake 31 – Wrong domain name, see p. 62

21 | Unsecure servers

<table>
<tr><td>The mistake</td><td>Design</td><td>Marketing</td><td>Strategy</td></tr>
</table>

You might think every website is under attack if you read the accounts of hacking in the press. Attacks on company websites are rare. But low-security sites that don't expect to be targeted can easily be picked out by automated software and vandalised or defaced.

> In a survey of over 300 UK Internet businesses, over 50 per cent believed they had adequate security measures in place, when their systems were actually insufficient.
>
> *Source*: Safeonline/MORI, March 2001

It is important to have procedures in place to cope with any potential attack as, theoretically, the hacker could even be one of your competitors. Often the investment occurs too late, after a site has fallen victim. As hackers develop new viruses and methods of attack, sites can never be 100 per cent safe but they need to minimise the risk – just one publicised attack can quickly destroy consumer confidence.

The solution

Hacking
Corporate **firewalls**, which surround your website and systems, are an excellent prevention mechanism but, if they are poorly configured or have ports/access points left open within them, they can be hacked. IT staff must employ detection and reporting software, regularly update servers with fixes to new viruses and should avoid storing personal and credit card details on the same server as the website.

Denial of service
More common than traditional hacking, denial of service attacks exploit weaknesses in Internet traffic networks by remotely bombarding your site with so much data that it overloads. Yahoo!, Amazon and CNN have all suffered such attacks. Again, proper configuration and monitoring of your **firewall**, and installing regular software fixes, minimises the risk. It is also believed that software to launch such attacks on mobile-phone networks is being developed.

42

Internal attacks

In the MORI survey mentioned on p. 42, almost 50 per cent of respondents said security breaches were most likely to come from their own staff. This can be prevented by having procedures in place to limit access to IT systems, especially when staff leave. You should also spread responsibilities so they don't rest with just one individual.

Testing

An ideal way to spot weaknesses is to try and hack your own site – some software and fraud consultancies offer this service.

Web host

Whether you hold your physical server in-house or with an external web host, you need to ensure access to it is limited, although you're unlikely to need the high-security bombproof rooms major banks use to store their servers.

Finally, if you want to convince management and staff of your system's security you could aim to comply with international online security standard ISO 17799 – although this can be costly to achieve.

Further information

www.iso.ch (International Standards Organisation)
www.cybersource.com (software developer specialising in fraud protection)
Hacking Exposed (useful book by McClure et al)
Mistake 68 – Lack of load testing, see p. 136
Mistake 43 – Unreliable web host, see p. 86

22 Poorly integrated online and offline services

The mistake

Online consumer preference for dealing with traditional retailers, is as much to do with them having both an online and offline presence, as it is to do with brand recognition. The ability to integrate 'clicks and bricks', will be a key method of future differentiation for many retailers and it is estimated that consumers who use both online and offline channels already spend up to a third more than those that shop in single channels alone.

VERY VERY IMPORTANT

> A global survey of over 11,000 consumers showed that 70 per cent prefer to use the Internet for research but then make the actual purchase offline.
>
> *Source*: American Express, Oct. 2000

Major retailers still separate their online and offline services. Some have been launched as separate companies and, although this might indemnify the offline company from the troubles of its online partner, consumers do not see the distinction. Online-consumer preference is likely to turn to those retailers that can present themselves as one integrated company, and provide the service and convenience to match.

The solution

Consumers are demanding integrated services in the following areas:

Payment, delivery and returns

Consumers need to be able to choose between home delivery or store pickup, which also allows them to pay by cash or cheque. Catalogue-retailer Argos, for example, allows online customers to check stock availability in their local store and then reserve it for collection. They also have a clear store-returns policy on their home page. Giving a physical location and access to people for in-store returns helps to create trust.

Product information and brochures

If consumers are using the Internet to research, then sites must have detailed and clear product descriptions. Conversely, **pureplay** retailers, such as health-store Think Natural, also recognise the importance of putting a physical brochure in customers' hands to drive traffic back to their website.

VERY IMPORTANT

Pre-ordering

Those that do research online can be offered reservation services to ensure their time isn't wasted when they get to the offline store. For example, the British Airport Authority's website allows travellers to pre-order both their parking and their duty free before they get to the airport.

The cost of integrating IT systems has been partly the reason behind the slow rate at which retailers are integrating their services, although those companies that have done so report the cost benefits of merged systems and data. Another reason is being unable to accurately measure how much custom offline is driven from online and vice versa. Employee incentives also need to be integrated, especially if you want to drive customers away from offline to online stores.

The key is to provide a consistent message to all consumers so they don't have to make a choice between shopping online or offline. As companies develop services across devices such as **WAP** phones and interactive TV, they need to see offline and online much more as part of a multi-channel strategy, rather than separately, in terms of 'new' and 'old' media.

Further information

www.argos.co.uk
www.thinknatural.com
www.baa.co.uk
Mistake 42 – Poor advertising integration, see p. 84

23 Unreliable fulfilment

The mistake   Design   Marketing   **Strategy**

The e-fulfilment process is diverse and includes handling **CRM**, payment processing, despatch and delivery, the controlling of stock levels and managing re-ordering systems. A company needs to get every one of these factors right to ensure that the fulfilment process is seamless.

Customer expectations are very different from those of the high-street shopper and the speed and efficiency of the ordering and delivery systems are no exception. Customers even expect delivery to be quicker from online retailers than from mail-order companies.

There is also still an amount of distrust and scepticism from consumers in the fulfilment abilities of online retailers. Consumers need to have faith in the benefits of e-commerce technology including trust in the existence of physical delivery systems. A retailer who fails to deliver on time or to the correct address, manage customer enquiries about the status of their orders, bills incorrectly, or fails to be upfront about stock levels, will not easily be forgiven.

The solution

Outsource

There are an increasing number of specialist e-fulfilment companies. Forrester Research Inc. estimates that by 2003, up to 73 per cent of UK e-fulfilment will be outsourced. The benefits of using e-fulfilment providers include specialist knowledge, lower cost per transaction compared to the amount of investment needed to develop a bespoke in-house system and scalability given an increase of orders. Outsourcing also enables retailers to concentrate their efforts in other areas such as product or market expansion. Service level agreements need to be drawn up and the e-fulfilment house needs to be accountable for maintaining expected levels of service.

E-fulfilment companies include iForce, who provide fulfilment for lastminute.com and eBay.co.uk, m-box, who service superdrug.com and MetaPack who manage fulfilment for Boots-owned wellbeing.com. Smaller companies will want to use the services of carrier companies such as DHL or UPS.

In-house

Handling in-house may be a preferred option for companies who already have an order-management and delivery infrastructure set up. In-house fulfilment can mean that problematic orders are dealt with faster and more efficiently. Tesco.com is the world's largest online grocer and already had the web-ordering system and delivery infrastructure to cope with fulfilment in-house. It uses a fleet of vans, collecting goods from stores nationwide. Marks and Spencer also handles e-fulfilment in-house by adapting existing mail-order systems, although a third-party firm is used for delivery.

Above all, fulfilment is about managing customer expectations and being upfront about delivery times, costs, return policies as well as having clear customer feedback channels if something goes wrong.

Further information

www.iforce.co.uk
www.m-box.com
www.metapack.com
E-Commerce Logistics and E-Fulfilment (useful book by Bayles)
Mistake 22 – Poorly integrated online and offline services, *see p. 44*

Measuring advertising by click-through

Online advertising allows marketers to analyse the exact number of people who clicked on their adverts. However, the ease at which this can be measured has created too great a focus on **click-through rates** as a determinant of success. With average banner click-through now below 0.5 per cent, and the need to be more accountable, you can no longer rely on measuring click-through, if it does not directly impact revenue. In addition, just using click-through also ignores people who respond to your advert indirectly, by visiting your site at a later date.

VERY IMPORTANT

60 per cent of digital advertisers use direct response such as click-through rates to measure effectiveness.

Source: Jupiter Media Metrix Inc, June 2001

There are a number of alternative metrics you can use to measure the effectiveness of your online advertising more accurately, in particular those based on performance. This not only affects how you measure your campaigns but can also determine how you buy them as well.

The solution

Conversion

Post-click tracking is a technique that allows you to tag website pages to see where users go after they've clicked on your advert. Do they go through to purchase or register for one of your services? This allows you to measure success in terms of cost per acquisition, cost per registration or even cost per sale. If you advertise on one site and it produces high click-through, this might hide a low number who actually then go through to purchase. A further step is to capture the value of what they purchase, to get a direct measure of their profitability.

Indirect conversion

Research has shown that on some online campaigns, up to four-fifths of respondents don't click on the advert but come back to your site at a later point. This can be measured by using **cookies** on people who do see the advert, which can be recognised if they visit your site at a later point. Cookies can also recognise people who come back after the campaign has finished, giving a useful measure of the effect of online branding.

Drop outs

Using clicks to measure success can also be misleading as a click can register, even if a respondent goes elsewhere before the website page fully downloads.

As well as measuring the results of a campaign using these metrics, there are a number of sites and advertising networks (such as ValueClick) that will let you buy online marketing campaigns on the same basis. In this way you only pay for adverts that produce results. Cost-per-click measurement is valid for certain campaigns if you just want to drive traffic and awareness. However, as more companies question the value of online advertising, you will need to use measurements that link results to much more tangible benefits.

 VERY IMPORTANT

Further information

www.valueclick.com

Mistake 67 – Online advertising does not build brands, see p. 134

25 Low maintenance

The mistake   **Design**   Marketing   Strategy

If you've ever commissioned a website for your company, you will know how difficult it can be getting the finance to build it. Too many companies see the completed site as their goal, not foreseeing that ongoing maintenance of the site is the main expense.

VERY IMPORTANT

The problem is more acute for smaller businesses with limited staff and resources. Maintenance, or 'content management' is seen as a chore, the job often being given to junior members of staff. Companies can outsource updates to an agency, but making frequent small changes can be expensive.

Not budgeting for content management is false economy, as customers will not stay loyal if your site is stale.

The solution

Plan
During the first few years of your site, you should split your initial design and content-management budgets by roughly 50:50. Planning from the outset is essential for larger sites, which may need to integrate future content management into existing databases.

In-house or agency?
It will generally be a mix of the two. Large companies can afford staff to make *ad hoc* changes or can afford to buy-in content-management software, but may need agencies for bigger projects such as **microsites**. Small companies should try and do as many minor changes in-house to minimise cost. An agreed monthly maintenance budget with a local agency for larger updates may also be required.

Content management tools

VERY IMPORTANT

Are an ideal solution, allowing content owners (with no IT experience), to update predetermined areas of the site via an **extranet**. Large companies will need to bring in specialists such as Mediasurface or Vignette. Smaller agencies should also be able to build simple content web interfaces for any site, as part of the initial design. This should be considered when an agency pitches for your business.

50

Accountability
At least one employee should have an overview of content management. Individual departments should be encouraged to use tools to update their sections of the site themselves, although you should agree a formal process and be wary of giving them too much autonomy. A website affects an entire company, so individual departments need to buy- in to the idea of updating the site as early as possible.

VERY
VERY
IMPORTANT

Monitor
It is also important to monitor the most popular areas of the site and encourage user feedback. There is no point updating content on pages that no one is looking at.

Overall, don't be tempted to spend too much of your budget on the initial design leaving little for maintenance. If you do, you would be better off not investing your money in a site at all.

Further information

www.mediasurface.com
www.vignette.com
Web Content Management (useful book by Nakano)

26 Poor quality PR

The Internet has had a significant impact on public relations, but many companies (and their incumbent PR agencies) have yet to catch up. Press releases can be sent more quickly and more frequently than ever before. As a result, journalists now have to cope with information overload, with more low-quality, pseudo press releases.

VERY IMPORTANT

> 40 per cent of corporate sites fail to answer journalists' most basic information needs.
>
> *Source*: Nielsen Norman Group, April 2001

This is further evidenced in poorly designed PR sections of websites, even if a company has an otherwise strong PR strategy. The designs do not understand how journalists use the Internet, generally too text-and-graphics heavy and poorly maintained. A company is also unlikely to get a comprehensive online press-clippings service from their PR department, as is the case with traditional print media.

Getting online press releases right is important. Websites are now the first place journalists go for corporate information, and can be the deciding factor in whether they write about a company or not.

The solution

Plan

Planning helps create consistent messages for a company and its individual brands. Lead times online are significantly reduced so you need to be careful that you do not send out too much information at once – offline media, with longer lead times, will then have no incentive to reprint old news.

Look at your PR website

Journalists don't have time for long downloads or clever graphics. Ask yourself whether a journalist could come to your site and within twenty seconds work out who you are and what you do? 'e-PR' media packs, often downloadable as **PDF** files, are useful in providing more detailed corporate information. Clear personal contacts to your PR team are essential, as are pages that can be clearly printed.

VERY VERY IMPORTANT

52

Write succinctly

An obvious requirement, yet companies still have the tendency to copy their text-heavy offline press releases to their website. Journalists, like other web users, scan rather than read Internet pages. For email releases, the 'subject heading' is all the more important, as is personalising emails – generic **spam** emails will be quickly deleted. And given the speed at which information travels online, you only have one chance to get your copy right – it can be impossible to make corrections at a later date.

very important

Monitor

To monitor your online reputation you need a comprehensive web clippings service. PR departments generally do not have the resource to do this so it is best to outsource to a specialist agency such as CyberAlert or eWatch or use free clipping services such as Excite's NewsTracker.

very important

Global audience

Your online press releases now reach a global audience. Unless your site is regionalised, you have to consider how any message will impact abroad. Simple, focused and succinct messages are therefore all the more important.

Above all, journalists need to know that they can turn to your website at any time, and rely on being able to get quick and concise information, in order to meet their deadlines.

Further information

nt.excite.com

www.cyberalert.com

www.ewatch.com

www.nngroup.com/reports/pr (website design for PR, report from Nielsen Norman Group)

Mistake 83 – No competitive-intelligence strategy, see p. 166

Mistake 41 – Unprofessional copywriting, see p. 82

27 Undeliverable email

Design **Marketing** Strategy

The mistake

Companies with an email strategy will generally base it on regular mailouts such as newsletters or promotions. But, with every mailout, emails that don't reach the recipient are bounced back as undeliverable.

This is caused by customers changing their email address. On average, people have two to three email addresses and many have separate personal and work accounts. Corporate email changes the most often, made worse in recent years as workers move jobs more frequently.

> 41 per cent of email users changed address at least once in the last two years and 15 per cent did so two or more times.
>
> *Source*: NFO WorldGroup, Feb. 2001

Undeliverables are critical to effective email list management but most companies sometimes ignore them or accept that there is nothing they can do. But with large databases, this can mean losing hundreds even thousands of contacts at a time.

The solution

Address-change procedure

You need to ensure a simple procedure is in place for customers to change their email address. Companies sometimes hide the email update process as it usually permits registrants to unsubscribe. Promoting a separate address change form avoids this problem. Allowing customers to change address from a set date in the future also helps them plan in advance if they change jobs.

Auto reply

A mailout will return several types of undeliverable. This means that return emails must be checked, even though this can be a laborious manual process. Replies can include a customer's new address or indicate that your email was rejected as it was too large in file size (this really only happens if you send attachments, which are best avoided). Replies might also indicate that the recipient's mailbox was full or their email **server** was temporarily down. These addresses should not be automatically deleted because they are undeliverable. Checking each reply will also highlight simple typing errors when the customer inputted their email address, which can be corrected accordingly.

Offline channels

Undeliverable email addresses should be cross-checked with your offline database. If you have a customer's postal address you could send them a postcard reminder to ask them to update their email on your website. Alternatively you can flag their file so if they contact your call centre in the future, staff remember to ask for their new email address.

Address-change services

If customers change email address, they can notify central services such as ihavemoved.com. These send details of the change to all partner companies simultaneously, but are dependent on customers' active co-operation.

Email address churn may increase further as more people switch to **broadband** services and change their Internet service provider and email as a result. It may initially be time-consuming but companies need to invest in an email retention process, especially as the cost of the process is likely to be less than the alternative cost of acquiring thousands of new customers.

Further information

www.returnpath.net (undeliverable email management company)
Mistake 4 – Lack of an email marketing strategy, see p. 8

28 Mass personalisation

The mistake   Design   Marketing   **Strategy**

<u>Personalisation is seen as the key</u> to effective e-commerce and a path to better <u>targeting.</u> But, other than high-profile examples like Amazon, how many businesses are really practising it? With limited data and technological solutions, the result is often restricted personal data within standardised communications. This 'mass personalisation' does not work as customers are sophisticated enough to realise that the message isn't unique.

Personalisation often means monitoring customer behaviour and using the data to cross or upsell other products. But past behaviour isn't necessarily a good indication of future sales and it is all too easy to collect data and then not do anything with it. A misguided assumption can produce an inaccurate communication, which can quickly irritate customers. Personalisation is a vague term with many meanings but, even with significant investment, the process can only be effective if it has a thorough understanding of customer preferences.

The solution

Communications based on registration or form data tend to lead to mass personalisation as they ask customers for information rather than learning from their behaviour. The data quickly goes out of date so making assumptions becomes more risky over time. However, software that learns from past behaviour is also risky as it is usually based on limited data.

Lack of data is due to customer-privacy concerns. Customers are more at ease giving purchase rather than private information (e.g. asking for salary details benefits advertisers more than it does customers). There is a point where personalisation, particularly monitoring behaviour, becomes intrusive and companies need to avoid looking as if they are spying. <u>Being open about the process and allowing customers to opt-out, helps to engender trust</u>.

Focusing on personalisation should not be at the expense of other channels. Perceptions of mass communication are less likely if a human element is added, such as links to call centres or offline stores. Personalisation may not even be relevant if the sales strategy is solely based on cheaper prices to encourage repeat custom.

VERY VERY IMPORTANT

<u>An alternative is to customise rather than personalise.</u> Customisation puts customers in control of what they want and is used with <u>personal home pages</u>

on the major portals or with bespoke customer-designed clothing as offered by Nike and Levis.

True personalisation requires significant investment and integration of data from all areas of the business – out of reach of many small- to medium-sized companies. But it is this lack of investment that creates weak and mass personalised communication. In this case, it may be more cost-effective to reject a strategy of personalised content for all, and use the website to deliver customisation instead, or a higher level of customer service only for the most valuable, regular and loyal customers.

VERY VERY IMPORTANT

Further information

www.1to1.com (useful articles from the Peppers & Rogers Group)
www.builder.com/Business/PersonSpot (personalisation guide from CNET)
Mistake 3 – Lack of an eCRM strategy, *see p. 6*

29 Lack of a human face

One of the main problems with e-commerce is the lack of human customer service. Customers need friendly human reassurance, especially at the purchase stage, and immediate and relevant answers to their queries.

Companies are turning to virtual assistants to add a human face to their sites. Their designers claim up to 90 per cent accuracy with virtual assistants' answers, but they are only as good as their pre-programmed responses. If they are not implemented correctly they can be more annoying than helpful.

Adding a human touch means more than just adding a face to your site and can be achieved without human graphical representation.

The solution

Adding images of people is a simple yet effective way to give your site a much more personal feel. Characters are another possibility such as the butler from search engine Ask Jeeves. They are only effective for certain types of site, particularly business-to-consumer and may look out of place on business-to-business websites. Clear contact and telephone details are another simple solution.

As well as virtual assistants such as mobile phone network One2One's Yasmin or the virtual newsreader Ananova, integrating your website with your call centre is essential. This can be as simple as 'call-me' buttons placed strategically on your site, particularly during the purchase stage, and are used effectively by the likes of Dell.co.uk. They automatically call customers back at a preferred time, although you must be sure there are staff to answer the calls, or put time limits as to when the call-me buttons operate.

More recently companies, such as the Bass Hotels Group, have been experimenting with instant messaging, available from companies such as Live Person. This allows customers to type text queries and get instant live responses. Process and bandwidth issues mean that instant messaging can be slow but it is an easy service to add and can be four times less expensive per customer contact than traditional telephone calls. An extension of this service is assisted chat, whereby call-centre staff see the web page customers are using and can move around the customer's PC screen in real time. This requires considerable integration and budget.

You don't need to spend a fortune on virtual assistants. Simply adding more responsive telephone contacts and easy access to customer service can be enough to bring a degree of humanity to your site.

Further information

www.one2one.com
www.ananova.com
www.liveperson.com
Mistake 19 – Abandoned shopping carts, see p. 38
Mistake 9 – Lack of trust, see p. 18
Mistake 8 – Limited user feedback, see p. 16

30 Splash pages

Splash pages are 'welcome' pages, used as an introduction to a site before the home page. Used mainly to reinforce the site's brand they have little or no real content and either require users to click on them to proceed or redirect automatically after a few seconds.

In general, they are totally unnecessary as they interrupt the navigation. Users will on average wait only eight seconds for a page to load, so why make it more difficult to reach the home page by forcing them to download two pages? Splash pages discourage repeat visits and can confuse search engines. Despite this, companies, which are large enough not to need such brand reinforcement, continue to use splash pages. Many sites use **Flash** animations as their splash page which increases download speed and can disable the **browser** 'Back' button, amongst other problems.

Web surfers are very goal-orientated and have no patience for anything, especially content-free splash pages, that prevents them from accessing what they want.

The solution

Logos and brand features can easily be incorporated into a site to prevent the need for a splash page. If you feel you must have one then ensure it is optimised to be as small a file size as possible, to minimise download time. Adding a 'click-to-enter' button may sound obvious but new Internet users may not know what to do if presented with just a logo. To avoid annoyance to repeat visitors, you can also **cookie** their PC so the splash page only appears on their first visit. Flash introductions should always have a clear 'skip intro' button, visible throughout the animation.

Gateway pages are another form of splash page, often used by global sites that need to determine which country subsite users wish to visit. Again *cookies* should be used to prevent the gateway reappearing on subsequent visits. Alternatively, the site can default to one country with clear home-page links to other country sites. Sites with rich-media content or **plug-ins**, sometimes also use splash pages to ask users which version of the site they wish to see. Sniffer code can be used instead, which automatically displays the site in the correct format, depending on the user's PC settings.

Animated splash pages can be useful for pure entertainment sites where they help to set a scene but, in general, there are many ways to reinforce a brand – splash pages should not be one of them.

Further information

Homepage and Splashpage (lots of examples in this book by Danielson)
Mistake 33 – Inappropriate use of Flash, *see p. 66*

31 Wrong domain name

The mistake Design **Marketing** Strategy

Web addresses or 'domain names' are either generic words, company or brand names and are the starting point for online and offline marketing activity. It's never been more difficult to register a meaningful domain name, especially for a global marketplace. It is estimated that there are less than 10 per cent of dictionary words left for the .com top-level domain.

As a result, companies looking to buy a domain, find themselves either using their company name; paying over-inflated prices for generic words; battling with **cyber-squatters** who registered their name before them; or creating meaningless new brand names with what is left, which are often too long or have ambiguous spelling.

Your domain name can mean the difference between success or failure and companies need to apply a little common sense in their selection.

The solution

You're unlikely to find the right generic word (e.g. *cars.com*) for a new website or brand so consider recent trends in brand-naming. These include 'statements' (*letsbuyit.com*, *go-fly.com*); combining generic words with existing brands (*trafficthemovie.com*); adding prefixes or suffixes (*topjobs.com*) or complete obscurity (*egg.com* or *smile.co.uk* for online banks). Whichever you choose, keep it short and avoid the use of hyphens or ambiguous spelling, as it causes confusion. Consumers often just guess a company's web address so consider what they are most likely to try. Plus consider how the name reads and sounds internationally and if it is broad enough for future expansion.

You must also use consistent sub-branding. Should the KitKat website, for example, be kitkat.co.uk or nestle.co.uk/kitkat? That depends on the strength of the brand. Only strong brands should consider separately named **microsites** (e.g. *www.smoothlydoesit.co.uk* for Tetley's Bitter) – weaker brands will just confuse customers with this approach. It's also important to consider how you promote your address. You can set your site to recognise your address without the 'www.' (e.g. Virgin Mobile promote their site as *virgin.com/mobile*). Promoting the 'http://' before the address should be unthinkable.

A range of new domain names is on the horizon (such as .shop and .travel) and you can now register addresses in over 350 local languages – this will widen naming options. Finding a name is easier using search tools such as whois.net, which shows all available addresses which contain a key phrase. You should also consider Keywords from RealNames, which allows you to type your company or brand name straight into a **browser** with no 'www.' or '.com' at the end.

VERY
IMPORTANT

It is argued that domain names will soon be academic anyway, as the growth of mobile Internet devices such as **WAP**, will mean people access Internet content via menu choices rather than typing in a web address. It will be a long time before this approach dominates so consider the practicality of your domain name, before you spend large sums of money on promoting it.

Further information

www.realnames.com
www.vi.net/dnnw (useful 'domain name news watch' section)
Mistake 20 – Domain mismanagement, see p. 40

32 Lack of call-centre integration

The mistake

The majority of call centres have yet to integrate with their online offering. This explains the poor email-response times of many leading companies. For most, integration means coping with email. Even though email may only account for less than 10 per cent of all contacts, the volume can be overwhelming. Email is more complex and there is a fear that it leads to a long back and forth dialogue, which reduces overall performance rates.

There is also the general misconception that online communication will replace the call centre and lead to a loss of jobs. Add this to the rise in dot com company closures, and many managers are left feeling hesitant. As a result, it is estimated that by 2004, less than a quarter of call centres will be web-enabled. But, in the meantime, online customers are left with poor service levels.

The solution

There is a range of integration options currently available:

- Email – including sending images, e-brochures and video attachments.
- 'Call me' buttons – which are placed on web pages and call back customers at a specific time by re-routing to the call centre.
- Instant messaging – allows live text chat between online customers and staff, although it can take over twice as long to complete than a phone call.
- Voice-over Internet – customers with the right software can talk to call-centre staff over the web.
- Avatars – virtual customer-service staff which respond to website text questions, although they often struggle with complicated queries.

Costs vary: a 'call-me' button is under £100 to set up, whereas an avatar will cost tens of thousands. Which you use will depend on customer demand, product and profit margins.

A major concern is that multimedia reduces productivity. We write email ten times more slowly than we speak, for example. How do you measure productivity if staff get a phone call one minute and an email the next? The traditional performance metrics of call volume and speed therefore need to be re-appraised. For example, the website can be used as a knowledge base to help customers answer the most common or mundane questions themselves (e.g.

using frequently asked questions), leaving the call centre to spend more time with high-value customers.

Call centres also require staff with different skillsets. They need to be email copywriters as well as good over the telephone and this variety helps to reduce staff turnover. Integration is about giving customers a choice. You might think the demand for options such as instant messaging does not justify the investment but the same was said of email fifteen years ago and now most call centres cannot cope with the volume.

Integration really means a cultural change. Multimedia call centres are rather 'contact centres' that improve service levels, job variety and quality. Companies need at least to make steps towards integration – they may have little choice in the future as customer expectations change.

Further information

www.cca.org.uk (Call Centre Association)
www.callcentermagazine.com (US publication with interesting features)
Mistake 8 – Limited user feedback, see p. 16
Mistake 5 – Email response time over six hours, see p. 10
Mistake 4 – Lack of an email management strategy, see p. 8

33 Inappropriate use of Flash

Macromedia Flash software is described as the professional standard for producing high-impact web experiences and it can be used to create superb animation effects online. It is for this reason, and the need to create something unique, that Flash is widely used, or rather misused on the web.

As a result we see meaningless animated logos and graphics which put style and concept before function. The worst is the often used Flash 'intro' which welcomes you to a site. On slow modem connections, this can cause users to leave your site prematurely. Flash can make your whole site more of a presentation or even commercial, reducing users' control over what they do online. The Flash player is also a **plug-in** and, although a version is already installed in over 95 per cent of PCs, less than 65 per cent of European users have the latest versions. Furthermore, Flash can render the 'Back' **browser** button useless, and more recent versions are incompatible with some Internet TV set top boxes.

Flash can be ideal to improve online branding but animated logos can be distracting. Sites such as coke.com and jaguar.com were still using Flash 'intros' and site navigation in 2001, when their brands are already well-established. The perils of too much animated content were clearly demonstrated with the original demise of the sportswear retailer Boo.com in 2000 – a site with great graphics that users found slow and difficult to use. Flash is not the problem – it's the way it is applied.

The solution

Determine your goals

Your site's goals and user base will determine to what degree you use animation and Flash. Information and e-commerce sites would do well to ask whether it really improves customer communication. Entertainment sites will find Flash a great way to interest users, especially if users have a high bandwidth connection.

Give Flash content its own area

If you do use Flash content, housing it in a separate area of your site allows users to choose if they wish to try it, rather than it being forced on them, such as with Flash 'intro' pages. Putting Flash content in **pop-up** windows can also be used and solves the problem of the 'Back' **browser** button not working.

> **Look at your competitors**
> Look at successful e-commerce sites such as easyjet.com or amazon.com. You are unlikely to find any Flash content.

Monitor navigation

If key areas of your site do use Flash, they often need their own specific navigation system. This should be logical, as there's a tendency for designers to create their own navigation, which is inconsistent with the rest of your site.

Above all, consider the cost of designing content, **microsites** or even whole sites in Flash. Could limited resources be better spent elsewhere, such as improving email communications or fulfilment?

Further information

www.macromedia.com/flash (excellent usability guidelines section)
Mistake 58 – Animation over information, see p. 116
Mistake 56 – The wrong plug-in, see p. 112
Mistake 30 – Splash pages, see p. 60

34 Free content

The mistake

The Internet revenue model of providing free content in return for advertising or e-commerce has come under much pressure since 2000. Non e-commerce sites that rely on advertising have seen reductions in incomes, making the free-content model unsustainable for many companies.

The perception that the Internet has always been free is changing. Although Internet Advertising Bureau research shows the Internet as the fastest growing advertising medium, it is a mistake to see this model as sustainable for all companies. It is also a mistake to assume that because content has historically been free, users will never pay for it.

The solution

Site owners are cautious about charging for online content but there are signs that this approach will work.

VERY IMPORTANT

> An average of 57 per cent of consumers would pay for appropriate online content.
> *Source*: ICM Research/Mondex International, May 2001

Look for free. Pay for printout ?!

The *Wall Street Journal* is one of the few online subscription-based news services heralded as a success. In the UK, *The Times* was the first newspaper to add a cost for online content, charging an annual fee for the use of their crossword, although they also offered a very basic crossword for free. The solution is to continue to offer a free service but to charge only for premium content that users value – in particular sports, entertainment (especially live webcasts) and specialist advice, such as financial.

The difficulty is deciding on what your users value and comparing it with the competition, which will always offer free content in one form or another. When Yahoo started charging for selling items on its auction service, auction listings fell by an estimated 90 per cent. There will need to be a testing period and established brand names will be in a good position to lever more value out of their content.

Another major difficulty is the lack of a suitable micro-payment system, which would make it easy for users to pay for content *ad hoc*. It is more difficult to make them pay upfront for an annual, higher-value subscription. Payments via mobile phone billing and e-wallets are one possible alternative. Content that is

VERY IMPORTANT

free still needs to maximise advertising revenue hence creating more personalised content will allow site owners to charge more for access to highly targeted user groups. Site owners are also looking at other ways to diversify revenue streams, including licensing technology or software to other businesses.

Companies should also look at the success of other pay for services. i-mode, the Japanese wireless service that offers free and pay-for content, already has 50 per cent of its users paying for information services. Although i-mode's barriers to entry are higher than the Internet, users are paying an average of US$2.50 per month. Conversely, UK news provider Teletext withdrew its sponsored **SMS** mobile-messaging service in Spring 2001, claiming the business model was fatally flawed.

The transition to pay for content will occur eventually, as it did in the television market with the introduction of cable and satellite. Content-based sites need to add subscription services, not only to weather market downturns but in preparation for wider uptake of **broadband**, when the quality of premium content will become much more appealing.

Further information

www.iabuk.net
www.wsj.com

FREE CONTENT?

The Internet has created a network for quick and free distribution of content, information and computer code. It is easy to copy, download or print out any web page. In many cases, this can infringe the content owner's copyright and potentially their revenue stream.

Between 1999 and 2000, online copyright infringement increased by 105 per cent.
Source: Net Searchers Net Protection Survey, 2000

Current legislation is unclear and fails to protect content owners adequately. It is made more complicated as the Internet cuts across geographic boundaries and their relevant laws.

The solution

There are a number of areas where a website-owner's copyright can be infringed:

Page design
The code that makes up your web pages is your copyright. Unscrupulous designers have been known to copy the source code of another website and modify it slightly for their own design.

Licensed content
Sites use registration, password protection and pre-payment systems to protect downloadable content such as reports or photographic images. There are technological solutions such as software that can add a watermark to pictures. Or software which controls how users view content (such as read but not print). However, this solution requires users to download a **plug-in**.

Domain names
Companies have greater protection against **cyber-squatters** who register corporate or brand names if they infringe an already registered trademark.

Metatags
Metatags are keywords used in the code of each web page to improve their search-engine ranking. Another company, possibly a competitor, could copy your

metatags, brand names or trademarks to improve their ranking, by using them in their own metatags.

Links

Although a web address is not copyrightable, if you link to another site and use **frames** to surround the content, or strip out any of the original page (such as the advertising) it may be seen as passing off the content as your own. 'Deep linking' to pages deep within another site may also infringe copyright.

Anti-corporate sites

Sites such as britishscareways.com, set up by disgruntled customers, can infringe copyright or trademarks if they use your logos or content. It is on this basis that many have been forced to shut down.

VERY IMPORTANT

Agencies

If an agency designs your site then you need to be aware that unless it is agreed in the contract, the agency can retain the copyright and potentially demand compensation if it is reused without their consent.

Policing

Checking the Internet for copyright misuse is time-consuming and difficult. However, online competitive-intelligence tools, such as domain name or online press monitoring will increase the chances of finding infringements.

The European Union addressed the issue in spring 2001 with a digital copyright directive, which member states have eighteen months to implement. In the meantime, it is not just high-profile video and music publishers that can experience online infringement – every company needs to be aware of the risks.

Further information

www.netsearchers.com/survey
www.cla.co.uk (Copyright Licensing Agency)
www.wipo.org (World Intellectual Property Organisation)
Mistake 83 – No competitive-intelligence strategy, see p. 166
Mistake 77 – Deep linking, see p. 154
Mistake 77 – Deep linking, see p. 154
Mistake 54 – Anti-corporate websites, see p. 108

36 English-only content

English is no longer the predominant language on the Internet. Less than 50 per cent of Internet users now speak English and Forrester Research Inc. estimate only a third of Internet users will use English by 2005.

VERY IMPORTANT [handwritten margin note]

Understandably, research also shows that nine out of ten non-English speaking Internet users prefer content in their own language and it is estimated that users are four times more likely to buy online if they are communicated to in their own language. Yet, over three-quarters of web pages worldwide are still written in English.

> Only one in eleven large companies can respond appropriately to foreign language email queries.
>
> *Source*: WorldLingo/International Data Corporation, April 2001

Large companies fail to target global markets effectively due to a lack of strategic importance given to foreign-language sites. The failure to respond to foreign-language emails in WorldLingo's survey included major brands such as BP, Ford and Daimler Chrysler. Cost and, in addition, global payment systems also discourage smaller companies. Yet the benefits, even in just incremental revenues can be enormous.

The solution

Traditional sales channels and competitors will identify which countries you should target online. This is particularly important in the business-to-business market, which is predicted to be predominantly multilingual within the next five years. Your site-statistics package will also be able to identify traffic from other countries. Internet usage is growing worldwide but Asia, Latin America and China are key growth markets. Chinese web surfers mainly access local-language content and over a third have already bought online.

VERY IMPORTANT [handwritten margin note]

The first step is to translate your brochure-based site. This requires a human approach and there are a number of companies such as Globalsight or Trados.com who offer this service. A possible solution is an automatic **HTML** translator such as that offered by WorldLingo. However, the results are not 100 per cent accurate and do not take account of linguistic or cultural differences.

72

Reaching non-English speakers is more than text translation. You need to be able to respond to foreign-language email queries with either trained staff or automated translation programs such as Altavista's free BabelFish web translator, which gives staff the gist of the enquiry. You also need to register all relevant web addresses, now that local-language **domain** names can be purchased from domain-registrant Verisign.

Localised content also affects responsibilities within organisations. Foreign content can be maintained locally but should be managed centrally to ensure you don't lose control. Other key areas of consideration are global payment solutions (which can be purchased as 'bolt-on' software packages) and the issue of fulfilment.

Above all, creating a site for non-English speakers is a strategic decision. A survey at the end of 2000 by Globalsight showed that 62 per cent of FTSE 100 companies fail to see globalisation as more than just translation. The importance of English online is diminishing and companies need to think strategically as well as technically if they wish to make the transition to a global marketplace.

Further information

babelfish.altavista.com
www.worldlingo.com
www.globalsight.com
www.verisign.com
www.lisa.org (Localisation Industry Standards Association)

A website's home page is its store front and is vital, as users will base their decision on whether or not to stay on a site by what they see. The average user spends less than eight seconds making this decision.

VERY IMPORTANT

Sites tend to concentrate too much on brand and image rather than calls to action, or they push everything to the home page making it more difficult to pick out where to go next. Along with unnecessary 'splash' introduction pages or pages that take too long to download, it is unsurprising that the home page is also most sites' top exit page.

The solution

Purpose

The aim and unique selling position of a site should be clearly explained on the home page. This is essential for lesser-known brands, particularly those using obscure **domain** names. For example, clothes retailer haburi.com needs clearer explanation than madaboutwine.com or studentuk.com. This can be done with a short introductory text or brand tag line and should concentrate on the site's benefits not just its features.

Unwritten rules

It would be boring if all sites used a standard home-page template, but there are a number of 'unwritten design rules' that most follow which makes navigation more intuitive. These include:

- Use of company logo at the top of the home page – the logo also links back to home from anywhere else on the site
- Privacy policies, terms of use, jobs, advertising links at the bottom of the page
- Repeating the main navigation channels at the bottom of long pages
- Shopping-basket icons on the top right
- One-click boxes to register for email newsletters
- Use of flags to indicate local language content.

Signposts

The home page should also cater for two user types by using signposts to help them achieve their goals. First-time users will want general product information (often addressed with 'quick tour' pages), search, corporate information, help and contact details. Repeat users, however, will be more interested in what is new, or quick login to registered services. American Airline's site, aa.com takes this approach by allowing users to login, book flights or tour services direct off the home page. Signposts for users who want to 'window shop' or those that want to purchase should also be considered. The most important signposts should also be higher up the page, such as airline ryanair.com, which has the 'Book Now' link prominently displayed at the top left of every page.

The home page is a user's first impression of your site. Considering these points along with intuitive and logical navigation, will help to ensure that it won't also be their last.

Further information

Homepage Usability (book by Nielsen and Tahir)
Mistake 6 – Poor navigation, see p. 12
Mistake 55 – Poor product information, see p. 110

38 Cookie mismanagement

Cookies are text files that capture website user information, which is then stored on the hard-disk drive of their computer. They have long been a concern, especially amongst privacy campaigners, as the information can be stored without the user's consent.

However, used correctly, cookies are both anonymous and harmless. They improve the user experience through personalisation, such as remembering settings from past visits (e.g. language preference) or for pre-populating registration forms. They can't read users' hard disc drives nor transmit viruses, and they recognise an individual PC, rather than the individual using it.

Nonetheless, it is users' perception and, to some degree, fear of cookies that should be of concern. As a result, their use needs clear and careful management.

The solution

Use cookies that benefit the user so they don't have to enter information more than once. Most users will find it reasonable to accept a cookie from the site they are visiting, but may question those from third-party companies that use the same site, such as advertising networks. These third-party cookies are aimed at better targeting for advertisers and should also remain anonymous. Back in 2000, advertising network DoubleClick came under US federal investigation for planning to merge third-party cookie information with a separate database of user names, so the cookies were no longer anonymous.

You should, therefore, always have a clear and explicit statement on your use of cookies in your website privacy policy and offer contact details if any user has questions. Several companies have been caught out by failing to mention in their policies cookies that they have subsequently used, including an embarrassing case by the US online privacy association, TRUSTe. Internet Explorer 6 is the first **browser** to make provision for protecting users by requiring third parties (such as advertising networks) to send a P3P (Platform for Privacy Preference) with any cookie they try and serve. A P3P describes the company's privacy policy, and Explorer will automatically block any cookie that does not have one attached.

Cookies should never capture personal identifiable information, such as credit-card numbers as these should be stored on the site's **servers** rather than the user's PC. Users can set their Internet browsers to alert them if they are being served a cookie, although less than 5 per cent bother to do this. However, if you want to avoid alienating this group, you should set your system so it uses the same cookie throughout the site. This ensures that users don't get repeated cookie alert messages. The European Commission is currently considering how cookies affect privacy and may force sites to ask users to 'opt in' to their use. However, this could dramatically reduce levels of website personalisation.

Cookies are a matter of user confidence – they are becoming more widely understood and accepted but still need to be clearly explained and honestly used, if you want to maintain trust.

Further information

www.cookiecentral.com (privacy news and opinion)
www.w3c.org/p3p (Platform for Privacy Preference)
Mistake 97 – Hiding user policies, see p. 194
Mistake 13 – Ignoring the Data Protection Act, see p. 26

39 Bolt-on site tools

The mistake	Design	Marketing	Strategy

Site designers are regularly reminded that a site with constantly refreshed content is the key to repeat visitors. The problem is that constant updating takes up a lot of resource.

Too often, the problem is solved by bolting on tools and features that at least make a site look dynamic. Tools such as newsfeeds, weather maps, search-engine boxes, webcams, wish lists, calendar reminders and comparison tools. These are often free from content providers, who gain both branding and traffic in return for licensing their content. Their use is partly fuelled by the success of affiliate programs – suddenly every other website wants to sell you a book from Amazon.

> A US survey of online shoppers showed that search and product information are more important than 'bells and whistle' features such as wish lists.
>
> *Source*: PriceWaterhouse Coopers, March 2001

Using these tools to add credibility, or because competitors or big brand names are using them, results in a loss of focus and can distract users. It makes sites look too much like portals or masks a lack of real, useful information. Content is indeed king, but it also has to be relevant.

The solution

Choose your tools carefully – they must add value to the customer experience. Search engine Google offers a toolbar, which integrates into the top left of your Internet **browser** – a great feature that makes search easier and more accessible. Yet, do customers really want to send e-greetings cards from an electrical retailer, such as jungle.com's 'j-Greetings'?

Where relevant, tools should also speed up the buying process. For example, britishairways.com's use of 'call me back' buttons links the buying process to a human voice in the call centre. Just because a tool is new or clever doesn't automatically make it right for your site. Entertainment is often a reason quoted for adding these tools but, if your site sells flights, for example, do your users really need to be entertained as well? There is also a tendency for companies to copy tools particularly if competitors use them – it's no coincidence that most major online booksellers all encourage reader reviews.

Before adding tools it is also wise to get the basics of design and service right, otherwise the tool may frustrate users. In addition, you should monitor tools' success and if they don't work remove them. Don't leave them up just because your competitors are using them.

Using website tools is about balancing content, design (especially your designers' imagination) and practicalities. Site tools or smart features might look good, but if they don't add value, don't use them.

Further information

www.toolbar.google.com
www.moreover.com (example of a popular news' feed tool)

40 Broad campaign planning

The mistake **The mistake** | Design **Marketing** Strategy

VERY VERY IMPORTANT

As an advertising medium, the Internet is unique in that it is entirely measurable. The perception is that you can easily target niche markets and, unlike other media, instantly optimise your campaigns in real time, effectively removing wastage.

The reality is different. The majority of media owners do not have sophisticated enough **CRM** or personalisation technology to offer advertisers such a high level of targeting. As a result, advertisers base their campaigns more on site content rather than the actual user.

VERY IMPORTANT

With falling **click-through rates**, rich-media advertising such as **superstitials** have become increasingly popular. Yet the double-digit click-through rates they can achieve, can be as much the result of their novelty and intrusion on the user experience, as on better targeting. Increasing choice means that online advertisers need to be ruthless about exactly where they spend their budgets.

The solution

The brief

The written brief to your media buyer is vital. You need to include details of your target demographic, competitor activity and overall marketing strategy. Be explicit about your objectives. Is your campaign to drive traffic, registration, sales or branding/awareness? You'll also need details of the advertising creative and how it will fit in with the plan, especially if you're using rich-media options.

Media owners

A site should provide you with not only detailed demographics of its users but also break down demographics into its various content channels. Although you might have difficulty getting detailed demographic breakdowns for **WAP** or handheld devices, given a lack of research. If you have a limited budget then it is preferable to concentrate on a few particular sites rather than trying to spread your message across too many.

Optimisation

If your adverts are served via a third party (which feeds your advert to all websites from one central location) then you can tweak your campaign as it progresses – such as targeting by time of day, content channel and capping how often a user sees your advert. You can also optimise response by creating several versions of your advert, which can be targeted at different sites, channels and time periods. Some media owners can also recognise different types of visitor (e.g. new visitors, those that have bought from the site, those from abroad) by using **cookies**, and this allows you to create more personalised adverts for each of those groups.

Post-campaign analysis

Media owners generally only get one chance to prove that their site can generate a response. So study their post-campaign reports carefully and, if possible, opt for post-click tracking which monitors what users do after they reach your site. A relatively low click-through from a website might hide a subsequently high number of absolute registrations or sales.

With the market downturn for advertising since 2001, advertisers are in an excellent position to bargain below the **ratecard** with media owners. Packaged deals in particular (e.g. banners, sponsorship, emails, handheld devices) are an ideal way to counteract the lack of true targeting possible online, and to get the most out of every campaign.

Further information

Mistake 65 – Over-use of banners, see p. 130
Mistake 24 – Measuring advertising by click-through, see p. 48

41 Unprofessional copywriting

The mistake	Design	Marketing	Strategy

Text is still the predominant communication method online. With Internet users viewing hundreds of pages every month, they have little patience for copy that does not get to the point.

The job of writing web copy, especially in small- to medium-sized enterprises, often falls to marketing, or in some cases IT staff. Even larger companies employ or outsource copywriters with insufficient online experience. The result is long pages of text, which do not appreciate how users read the web or help them find what they want. Professional writing is also essential to online promotions, such as email.

Writing professional web copy will also help you to avoid other key mistakes, by aiding navigation, usability and minimising page-download speed. It becomes even more important if you extend your offering to the mobile or handheld markets, where succinct copy is critical given the size and connection speed of devices.

The solution

Budget for a copywriter

They are often the last consideration when setting online budgets. Don't necessarily use your current marketing department or agency – choose an agency with online copywriting experience. In the absence of a good online copywriters' directory, freelance marketing recruitment agencies can be a good place to look.

Write concisely for your audience

VERY IMPORTANT

The majority of users don't read web text – they scan. If it's not relevant, they move on. There's no room for details, especially higher up the navigational structure of your site. As a rule, write under 50 per cent of what you would write offline and get straight to the point.

Break up your copy

Use headings, highlighted text, lists and bullet points. This makes copy easier to scan.

Link for more detail

Links should be used to supplement your copy and provide more detail for those who are interested. Limit the number of links used and keep them relevant. For detailed copy such as reports, it is better to offer these as downloadable documents such as **PDF** format.

Summarise

VERY IMPORTANT

A one-sentence summary can be enough for users to decide whether to read on or link elsewhere – an aid to simple navigation. Newspapers have used this 'conclusion first' approach successfully for years. Summarising the content of your links can also help users quickly decide where to click next.

Graphics

Don't add graphics for their own sake unless they are appropriate to the copy. Pictures can also say enough to allow you to cut back on explanatory details.

Review

Web copy is increasingly customers' first impression of your company and can be online for months, even years. So get someone other than your copywriter to check it before it goes live – ideally several of your users.

Further information

www.gooddocuments.com

www.adassoc.org.uk (lists recommended reading from the Advertising Association)

Mistake 51 – Careless email copy, see p. 102

42 Poor advertising integration

There are an ever-increasing number of digital platforms reaching a wider audience – such as websites, mobile phones, interactive TV and handheld computers. The importance of integrating advertising and marketing activity across these platforms is well-documented but, in practice, many companies are just paying lip service to the concept.

VERY IMPORTANT

> Approximately half of companies admit that their website does not integrate effectively with their offline marketing activity.
>
> *Source*: NewWorld Commerce/*Marketing Week*, March 2001

The most common error is that offline media (e.g. television or direct marketing) leads the design process, often because they have the lion's share of the budget. Their ideas are then simply re-purposed to work online. Integration means more than re-purposing and online needs to be involved from the start.

The solution

Creative

Internal or external design agencies must meet from the outset to work on integrated campaigns to avoid re-purposing. Online activity is unique in that it is interactive, so can extend a brand built initially offline by bringing it to life. For example, when Persil launched its new washing capsules, creative across platforms followed the same theme, although web and interactive TV campaigns allowed users to take part in fun chat and games.

Call to action

VERY IMPORTANT

Every advert has a call to action. Even those which are 'pure' brand awareness with no contact details, have an implicit call to action. Websites are perfect tools for this and are more easily remembered and more cost-effective than telephone numbers. Car advertisements are notorious for not making the most of web calls to action. The web address usually appears for a few seconds at the bottom or end of television adverts or in small text at the bottom of posters, so that it is hardly noticeable.

It is also important to match the website to the campaign creative. This means creating **microsites** with consistent branding rather than using the home page as the call to action (e.g. www.va-va-voom.co.uk for the launch of the new Renault Clio). The microsites should in turn have further calls to action and the opportunity to capture data.

Media choice

With so many media to choose from, assigning budgets needs to be more than arbitrary. The only way to achieve this is through research and measurement. Research will determine customers' platform preferences and how they respond. Measurement requires comparison across platform (e.g. cost-per-acquisition of online versus direct-marketing campaigns) and subsequent adjustment. Although it is much harder to quantify the effect of TV or poster versus online in terms of branding.

VERY
IMPORTANT

Online is just one part of the marketing mix along with other forms of communication, but it is unique in its ability to cost-effectively interact with consumers. With consumers constantly bombarded by more marketing messages every day, consistent integrated campaigns are the best way to widen audience reach and mean more than just putting the company web address on everything.

Further information

Mistake 22 – Poorly integrated online and offline services, see p. 44

43 Unreliable web host

Your web host or 'Internet service provider' is a fundamental part of your e-business strategy. Resources spent designing and marketing your online offering will be wasted if your web host is slow and unreliable – even thirty minutes **server** downtime can cost thousands of pounds in lost revenue.

VERY IMPORTANT

Only 14 per cent of websites in the UK, Asia Pacific and the US use a web-hosting company, and many are unclear as to the benefits of offsite hosting.

Source: Ovum Research, May 2001

Given the cost of qualified staff, it is generally more effective to outsource **hosting**. However, it's easy to choose the wrong host given the tremendous choice and range of packages on offer. Small businesses can pay for more than they need on packages with inappropriate frills, whereas larger sites can find a good-value host very costly if service and scalability is poor.

Although there is a big difference between hosting a small website and a high-traffic e-commerce site, it is very much a market where you pay for what you get. Data storage is cheap, expertise and service is not.

VERY IMPORTANT

The solution

To feel confident in your choice of host, make sure you take the following into account:

Size

Most sites of around a hundred pages can fit within 5MB of server space. So consider how much space you really need before signing up. Importantly, the cost of growth (usually measured per **megabyte**) should be determined as your site expands or uses more rich-media content.

Speed

This is determined by your host's bandwidth and the number of other clients on each server. Find out how many clients share your server – there should be around 50 per cent spare capacity. Larger sites should invest in their own dedicated server, which can be leased from your host.

Reliability

Your host should guarantee at least 99 per cent server uptime, ideally over 99.5 per cent. It is difficult but preferable to get a service-level agreement signed, which includes penalties for prolonged downtime.

Support

If you are on a budget, you need to watch your host's true level of support. You need 24-hour, email and phone access, especially if your site targets customers across different time zones.

International

If you have a global operation you should consider hosting in more than one country (such local 'mirror sites' can improve access speed). US hosting can also be much cheaper.

Other

Your host should also offer adequate security (e.g. **SSL**) to prevent hacking or access to credit-card data; daily back-ups (although you should do this yourself as well); other server applications such as standard shopping cart or database functionality; at least basic site statistics – and support multiple operating systems (such as Unix, Linux or Windows NT).

Further information

www.nsiratings.com (tested list of European web hosts)
www.uk-hosting.org.uk (useful guide to hosting)

44 No web presence because of cost

The most common reason for small businesses not having a web presence is lack of knowledge and budget. The average small to medium-sized business can spend over £20,000 a year on e-commerce, which is out of the sights of much smaller enterprises, who would benefit the most from a website. It is estimated that just under 50 per cent of UK small businesses have a website and two-fifths do not yet have Internet access.

VERY IMPORTANT

> Only 21 per cent of businesses with fifty employees or less, use the Internet to sell online. Of those, 60 per cent use email or a basic web form rather than secure e-commerce facilities.
>
> *Source*: Actinic Ecommerce Report, 2001

For small businesses, particularly sole traders, it is a lack of understanding of the real costs involved which prevents them going online. Yet, there are a wide range of low-cost web solutions targeted at small businesses, many hosted by leading solutions providers. Many also include e-commerce and transaction software. Even if they are just brochure-based sites, they can help generate leads and deal with enquiries more efficiently. Although successful e-business requires investment, it is possible to set up a small and effective brochure site for a few hundred pounds or an e-commerce operation for just a few thousand.

The solution

Software packages

Off-the-shelf e-commerce packages such as Actinic Catalogue or Shop Factory provide shopping-cart solutions for just a few hundred pounds. These are only relevant for small businesses that are prepared to and have the expertise to do the design-work themselves. They can also be easily integrated into some of the many web-design packages like Microsoft FrontPage.

Low-cost agencies

As well as local design agencies, companies such as Virginbiz.net, or BT Web Design have small-business web solutions, which often include free trials. Some of the UK's high street banks, e.g. Lloyds TSB, also offer solutions. These solutions include web **hosting** and are sold as easy to set up and complete packages.

Free software

Freeware and shareware portals such as shareware.com or download.com have a huge amount of free downloadable software and utilities that can be used to design and promote any site and would be equally useful to much larger organisations. Some of the free software lacks advanced features or requires the user to view advertising, but otherwise is very useful.

Actinic's Ecommerce Report 2001 also showed that small businesses that did engage in e-business benefited from their investment. Over half of web store owners rated their store as very or extremely successful. Of those that were profitable, over 70 per cent achieved profitability in the first six months of operation.

Overall, if a small business has the skill, time and resource to purchase the individual software packages itself (website, **domain** name, hosting, e-commerce software) then costs can be reduced. But, even without this knowledge, lack of budget shouldn't be used as an excuse for not going online given the wide range of low-cost solutions available.

VERY IMPORTANT

Further information

www.actinic.co.uk
www.shopfactory.co.uk
www.bt.com
www.lloydstsbcardnet.com
Mistake 74 – Choosing the wrong web-design agency, see p. 148

45 Lower online prices

The Internet has developed a focus on lower prices and many retailers believe consumers demand that products online should be cheaper than offline. Historically, start-up companies with undeveloped brands used low prices to differentiate themselves from traditional offline stores, given much lower overheads. The popularity of price-comparison search engines such as shopsmart.com or kelkoo.com have also fuelled this perception.

It is a misconception that online prices must be cheaper than offline, even if this is possible given the cost savings of online distribution. If site usability, service and fulfilment do not live up to expectation then consumers opt for more trusted brands, even if their prices are higher.

The solution

Consumers appreciate the time saved by shopping online and, if serviced correctly, are willing to pay for it. This is why a shopper will buy a single lower priced item online, which by the time delivery charges are added may cost more than if they bought it in their local high street. Research also shows that those who do not yet shop online give convenience higher importance than those who currently do.

In some markets, a low-price strategy can alienate existing offline distribution channels or even offline customers. In 1999 Delta Airlines famously placed a $2 penalty on any tickets not purchased online, only to remove it two weeks later after consumer uproar. This inconsistency explains why retailers with strong offline channels prefer to use coupons or loyalty points rather than price, if they want to discount online.

VERY IMPORTANT

Online shopping continues to grow despite the fact that online prices are also rising. The Goldfish ePI online consumer price index measures monthly UK price changes. Between November 2000 and May 2001, for example, the price of a typical online shopping basket increased by 3.5 per cent (which was above the price index for offline goods). Interestingly, **pureplay** retailers' price rises were a third higher than traditional 'clicks and mortar' stores.

McKinsey & Co further explained the effect of rising online prices with a study in March 2001. It showed online prices could rise within a certain range, by as much as 17 per cent, with a negligible effect on sales. Although some industries varied (financial services could only sustain a 1 per cent rise). Price rises are also easier to test online but must be managed carefully to avoid customer complaint. Growing competition and market consolidation is showing that a low-price strategy can only be achieved by the few and is more difficult for small companies or late market entrants.

As the Internet develops into a new era, consumers primarily shop online because of convenience. It is also now more difficult to counter the reduced profit margins of lower prices with online advertising revenue. Sites therefore need to look to better online experiences, service and fulfilment and translate these into higher and more sustainable pricing strategies, if they wish to keep customers longer than the next competitor's discount.

Further information

www.goldfishepi.com

Mistake 59 – Pricing errors, see p. 118

46 Lack of Internet business planning

The mistake   Design   Marketing   **Strategy**

In recent years, many companies, particularly small to medium-sized enterprises, have developed an Internet presence without really knowing why. The downturn in the industry has also produced a 'wait and see' attitude without a clear direction of where a site is going next.

> A survey of UK and German companies showed that 25 per cent said they had turned to e-commerce for short-term gains, whilst 50 per cent had no business plan to back up the move.
>
> *Source*: BT Ignite/MORI, May 2001

VERY VERY IMPORTANT

This indicates a lack of realistic planning. Executives are now finding it increasingly difficult to secure funding without a clear business plan that shows real return. An Internet business plan is similar to a traditional plan; however, it needs to take account of the unique nature of e-commerce and the associated costs involved.

The solution

A successful Internet business plan considers the usual elements of situation, goals and the process to achieve them but also needs to consider the following:

Objectives
Goals need to be focused on customer return in the case of e-commerce and customer service; or on cross-company return in the case of cost savings through distribution or marketing. It is no longer sufficient to aim to achieve higher site traffic or registrations, unless they impact directly on the business.

Competition
The speed at which companies innovate means that you need constantly to consider both **pureplay** and traditional competitors.

Marketing
If you're on a small budget it is easy to underestimate the cost of online advertising campaigns if you want them to drive a significant response.

The importance of a good host.

Otherwise, you need to build into your plan how you will leverage the most out of existing offline channels to promote your site.

Team
A website impacts on an entire organisation, so all departments need to buy into and contribute to the process. Giving departments a degree of ownership is vital in securing resource to keep the site maintained after it has been built. If you lack technical resource, particularly in website **hosting**, then you also need to compare the costs of in-house and outsourced development.

Budget
The main mistake companies make in determining their medium-term budgets is to underestimate the cost of ongoing maintenance. Over a three-year period, you may need to allocate up to 50 per cent of resource on maintenance alone. You also need to consider the cost of hardware, software, payment processes and integrating a site into any existing backend systems.

There are a number of software packages, such as Web Strategy Pro, PlanWrite and PlanIT, which will help with Internet business planning, and can produce formulaic plans.

Further information
www.webstrategypro.com
www.brs-inc.com (PlanWrite)
www.focusmm.co.uk (PlanIT)
www.bplans.com (useful guide to business planning)
 How to Write A .com Business Plan (helpful book by Eglash)

47 Lack of staff buy-in

The mistake   Design   Marketing   **Strategy**

The development of a successful Internet venture is not just the work of one department, as it impacts on an entire organisation. Early websites, which were nothing more than online brochures, were traditionally managed by marketing. But, as sites expand, they represent a much broader cross-section of a company.

For many staff, especially if the Internet plays no part in their lives outside work, a website may not be welcomed because it:

- Requires new ways of working and new skills to be learnt
- Creates additional work, particularly for those dealing direct with customers (e.g. email volumes)
- Can be perceived as a threat to jobs
- Is seen as a minority distribution channel compared to traditional ways of working.

VERY VERY IMPORTANT

Recent Internet failures and the falling price of stocks have also made senior management wary of taking risks, leaving them wondering where the hype ends and quantifiable returns begin.

The solution

Getting staff to buy-in to Internet projects means involving them from the start. In the initial design, staff, particularly those who deal directly with customers, should be consulted at key stages of development. By giving departments 'ownership' of their section of the website, they will be more interested in its future maintenance, rather than seeing content updates as a chore. In the final stages of development, staff as well as customers should be used for usability testing.

Ownership can be extended by using web-based content-management tools, so that departments can update the website themselves. One manager should oversee web development, ideally with no bias to any particular department. This can be achieved if the e-commerce team is set up as a separate division rather than part of IT, marketing or a joint working group.

New technology also requires new skills. For example, call centre staff have to become good email copywriters whilst human resources need to manage job applications by email. Companies such as PowerGen have taken this further

94

by offering all staff subsidised home PC rental and Internet usage (which also takes advantage of generous tax breaks). Customer feedback is another way to create buy-in. Positive feedback can easily be circulated around a company by email. Although reactive, underlining competitor online activity can also encourage staff buy-in and investment. Investment, however, must be backed up by quantifiable performance goals. These should also be shared, where possible, cross company, and can be used as part of bonus or incentive schemes.

 However, the key to success is like any other project – senior management buy-in. This does not just mean approval but creating a vision, shared amongst all employees, of how e-business will integrate across the entire organisation. Implementing an effective Internet strategy means more than just having a website or e-commerce facilities – it requires and should be measured on a real change in corporate culture.

Further information

Mistake 32 – Lack of call-centre integration, see p. 64

48 Creating unattainable expectations

The mistake

The poor financial and service performance of many e-businesses is as much a result of creating unattainable expectations as it is over-ambition. The need to outperform your competitors whilst racing down new business channels has created a culture of over-promise in advertising and customer communications.

Take Barclays online banking service, for example. In April 2001, one of their advertising campaigns was branded as 'misleading' after it claimed 24-hour access and showed an actor paying his bills in his pyjamas. In fact, the service shut down for a short period each night for maintenance. Communications for the benefits of **WAP** are another example. British Telecom was severely criticised for its millennial WAP campaign, inviting you to 'Surf the BT Cellnet'. It was said that the reality of WAP was not the 'mobile Internet' they suggested, but, rather, limited usability and re-purposed Internet content.

The solution

It's an old marketing adage to under-promise and over-deliver but many companies have forgotten this technique in the new economy. Exceeding expectations covers many areas discussed elsewhere in this book. However, there are several key points that should be considered:

Monitor
Use surveys, focus groups, site statistics and feedback to find out what your customers really expect. This is a continuous process as expectations change over time. Choose research companies such as e-Satisfy with particular experience in this field.

Be honest
Tell customers what will happen, not what they want to hear.

Ensure reliability

From page download times to **server** up time, reliability determines your customers' most basic impression of your company.

Only offer value-added features
Don't add 'bells and whistles' features to your site if you are yet to meet even the most basic of expectations. Users are less likely to use these features if they do not either add value or quicken the buying process.

Be responsive
There must be clear channels of feedback and customer service with a guaranteed speed of response.

VERY
VERY
IMPORTANT

Compare with offline expectations
Where appropriate, your online performance should exceed that of your offline – customers' expectations are more demanding online. It is estimated that 5 per cent of customers receiving poor online service will never subsequently visit your offline business.

Compare budgets
Finally, look at your marketing and **CRM** budgets. Is there a tendency to spend considerably more on saying what you can do, rather than actually doing it?

Further information
www.e-satisfy.co.uk
Mistake 9 – Lack of trust, see p. 18

49 Choosing the wrong web partner

The mistake

VERY
IMPORTANT

It is rare for an Internet company to be successful on its own. With reductions in Internet marketing budgets and falling online advertising response rates, partnerships are seen as a much more efficient way to build brand awareness and sales, particularly for small or young companies. Online partnerships can be set up quickly and help to spread both cost and risk.

However, it is estimated that between 30 and 50 per cent of partnerships fail. They can be difficult to manage, have been traditionally set up on the basis of generating traffic, without linking traffic directly to revenue, and performance is seen as difficult to measure.

Even if online partnerships are easy to initiate, they need to be carefully chosen, as failure can cost both financially and in terms of brand damage.

The solution

Online partnerships, whether partners are exchanging products or content, generally fall into one of several categories:

- Advertising/awareness – to place the brand in front of the partner's audience which would cost significantly more if purchased as straight advertising. Useful if trying to reach a global online audience. Smaller companies used to exchange equity as part of a partnership deal in return for this type of advertising but it is less common given the fall in the value of dot com stocks.
- Distribution – allows a partner to use the other partner's sales channels. Partnerships between **pureplay** and offline stores are a good example, e.g. ThinkNatural.com and retailer Superdrug. The pureplay also benefits from improved trust and credibility.
- Customer base – which is widened by combining both partners' databases.
- Defensive – to block the competition from forming the same partnership.

Checking competitors' deals is a good place to start looking for partners: it is easy to find out who is linking to competitors' sites by using tools such as AltaVista or Link Popularity. Whatever the type of partnership, both companies must compare competencies and have a complementary brand fit if it is to work. Sites are tempted to diversify if it is an incremental revenue stream but should avoid diversifying into unrelated products or services. One way to

VERY IMPORTANT

minimise any brand damage in case of failure is to launch partnerships as sub-brands or **microsites**, which are separate to the main website.

In addition to poor brand fit, lack of performance is the second biggest reason for failure. Therefore, a regular reporting mechanism must be set up and expected returns (e.g. visitors, e-commerce revenue) be agreed in advance. This should form part of the contract, as well as exit clauses and data sharing rights.

VERY IMPORTANT

Although a partnership should be a long-term commitment, the volatile nature of the new media industry means that short-term renewable contracts are preferable.

A partnership needs to show real return in terms of innovation and efficiency, and should be an essential part of every marketing mix.

Further information

LOOK AT →

www.altavista.com (type 'link:' followed by competitor web address to see who links to them)

www.linkpopularity.com

Mistake 18 – Not maximising strategic links, see p. 36

50 Damaging brand reputation

At the beginning of 2000, many Internet start-ups thought that building a brand was a result of advertising and awareness. But, as established companies expanded their Internet offerings, it became clear that image and identity are more than a smart idea and **domain** name.

VERY VERY IMPORTANT

Internet retailers have failed to realise that online brands are built less on traditional emotional ties and more on function and practicality. Amazon.com, for example, has built its brand on functional promises of 1-Click e-commerce and on-time delivery. Brand reputation can literally erode before customers' eyes if websites underperform. Just having a website is no longer enough.

The solution

Core brand values

Values should be clearly reinforced online, especially in terms of content and customer service. Detergent manufacturer Persil uses its website to underline its values of reliability and responsibility. The site is positioned as a 'careline' with guides to washing, stain removal and the environment. Cadbury's website has a 'Chocolate Encyclopaedia' underlining the long history of its products and brand.

Consistency

Consistency of message and visual identity must be the same across all platforms. For example, Carlsberg lager's strong offline association with football has an equally strong presence on its website.

Interaction

Interaction is key to online branding as it offers the opportunity to talk one-to-one to consumers and build relationships. This is why personalisation is seen as the key to effective online brand-building. For example, Guinness.com regularly uses competitions, video streams of advertising and interactive games to engage online visitors.

Brand extension

Extending a brand to non-core products can be more easily achieved online if values are already reinforced. Direct Line's online car retailer, jamjar.com, was able to more easily offer a car loan and insurance service in addition to direct sales given the company's history in financial services. However, it is wise to maintain focus. Although it is easier for a brand to diversify online, this doesn't mean it should be done, even if it does create additional revenue streams. Some companies have also achieved extension by linking with other more established brands. Lastminute.com and Thomas Cook's strategic partnership, for example, brings together a unique customer base with greater experience and brand heritage.

VERY
IMPORTANT

Subtle branding

Used particularly to reach a younger, commercially averse audience, subtle branding is being increasingly used online. Specialist websites or **microsites** associate the content and quality of experience with the brand, despite the brand presence being minimal. However, this only works with recognised established brands.

It is easy to simplify a brand online and underestimate consumer expectations, the worst damage occurring by not having a website at all. Even if a site has consistent and interactive elements, usability issues such as slow loading pages or poor navigation can also damage reputation. Whereas the Internet is an excellent vehicle for extending products and values, it needs careful management, as it is also one of the fastest ways to destroy years of carefully planned offline brand-building.

VERY
IMPORTANT

Further information

www.persil.com
www.cadbury.co.uk
www.carlsberg.co.uk
www.brandnet.co.uk (consultancy with interesting 'eLeague' brand reports)
Brand Building on the Internet (useful book by Lindstrom and Andersen)
Mistake 67 – Online advertising does not build brands, see p. 134

51 Careless email copy

The average worker sends and receives almost 200 emails a day and an increasing percentage of these are marketing or commercial messages. As email marketing is so cost-effective and responsive, any company can attempt it.

> Email users' top irritants include: lack of formal greeting or sign off; spelling mistakes; grammatical errors; and overfamiliarity. In addition, 82 per cent believe good manners matter on the Internet.
>
> *Source*: MSN/Debrett's, January 2001

Research by Northwestern University shows that business negotiations conducted electronically run into more difficulties than by phone. Although email advertising produces, on average, higher **click through rates** than banners, recipients are constantly looking for reasons to delete any email they see as irrelevant – so attention to detail is essential.

The solution

Subject line

Is the most important copy in any email and recipient's initial clue to your message. Keep the copy brief, using a maximum of thirty-five characters.

Content

Aim for concise copy: in general users will scan only two or three paragraphs before deciding on relevance. Writing succinctly, for example, with bullet points, ensures your tone is less likely to be misinterpreted. Abbreviations are best left to mobile text messaging campaigns. Personalised and timely copy produces a higher response but this will depend on the sophistication of your database. Also be careful with time-specific references, as you never know how long it may be before a user opens your mail. Use capital letters sparingly and always include clear calls to action, so users know what to do next.

Sign off

At the bottom of emails, should be minimised to five lines. Make it clear why users have been sent your communication and explain how they can update or unsubscribe from your database. Clear contact information should also be included.

Email attachments
Such as games, executable files and video clips are increasingly rejected by corporate firewalls, yet are increasingly popular with marketers. An analysis of your target database should clarify if you should use attachments. Avoid them if you are unsure or put content on web pages which users can link to. Links should always be preceded with 'http://' to ensure they are picked up by all email programmes.

Auto responses
Auto responses to email enquiries need to be carefully and generically worded. 'Email a friend' or viral emails whereby the content is automatically generated must avoid over-endorsement of a product as it can look as if the sender has written it himself.

Rich media
Video and **HTML** emails are now widespread, given better presentation and higher click through rates. To see if your audience can accept rich-media emails, user analysis is again essential, or employ 'sniffer' code, which can determine what format a recipient's email program can accept, and display the email appropriately. HTML emails need to take on the principles of web-page design and the temptation to fill out the page even if you have little to say should be avoided.

Spellcheck and test
Particularly important if you are sending bulk emails.
   Finally, you need to know when not to use email. Letters and phone calls can often solve problems (such as customer complaints) more quickly and cut down on subsequent email communications.

Further information

Mistake 41 – Unprofessional copywriting, see p. 82
Mistake 4 – Lack of an email marketing strategy, see p. 8

52 Not analysing site statistics

The mistake   Design **Marketing** Strategy

Every website records **log files** of user visits and most companies have some form of a statistics package to record the volume of traffic. Companies generally concentrate on top-level measurements. **Page impressions** or most visited pages are important for sites based on advertising revenue, whereas users and sales are more important for e-commerce sites. There is often confusion over the exact definitions of many web statistics as there are no defined standards and the volume of other data from **log files** can be overwhelming.

As a result, managers often lack the expertise or resource to get more than top-line figures and need to know what to look for in order to turn log-file data into more actionable information.

The solution

Most statistical software should be able to produce the following information, which can be used as part of wider business decision-making:

Paths through site
Indicates the sequences of pages and content channels that users follow. The paths of buyers highlights key information that can indicate navigation, promotion and customer-service improvements.

Top referrers
Show the sites from which visitors entered. This can indicate the success of advertising campaigns and pinpoint other sites for strategic partnerships.

Repeat visits over time
Give an indication of returning visitors and the 'stickiness' of a site.

Access by time of day
Shows traffic peaks and troughs which indicate the best time to target promotions, or can help plan staffing levels in knock-on departments such as call centres or order fulfilment.

Frequency and duration

Indicates the length of time visitors stay on a site as well as how often they return, giving a basic measurement of retention.

Top exit pages

Where visitors leave a site can indicate potential problems.

Geographic and system data

The location of visitors can indicate new foreign markets whilst system data such as users' **browser** versions and screen resolution can be captured and fed back to designers to ensure the site is fully compatible.

For management reporting, these figures can be calculated as ratios and compared over time. The most popular are:

- Sales conversion ratio: online sales ÷ **unique visitors**
- Click-to-buy ratio: average number of clicks until a user makes a purchase
- Buyer-to-browser ratio: number of buyers ÷ unique visitors
- Site penetration ratio: unique visitors to any key page on the site ÷ unique visitors to the home page.

The development of these metrics is a step towards making websites more accountable and linking them with more meaningful business information. Site statistics shouldn't be purely the domain of webmasters or technical departments but need to be communicated across an organisation and seen on a much more strategic level.

Further information

www.webtrends.com

www.netgen.com (software suppliers with information on getting the most from e-metrics)

Mistake 7 – Not measuring website ROI, see p. 14

53 Lack of community

The mistake   Design   Marketing   **Strategy**

The three key elements of e-business success have long been seen as content, commerce and community. Community is aimed at driving repeat visitors and loyalty but is an over-used and often misunderstood term. An online community is simply a meeting place where like-minded people discuss a common interest and is easier to join online given the lack of geographic boundaries.

Companies, particularly those that target niche demographics, can capitalise on this to build relationships and loyalty into their website. Community builds emotional ties with a brand, which helps to develop trust. But the very fact that the relationship is corporate means that community has to be very carefully managed.

The solution

Online, a community can be as much based on the traditional sense of the word (e.g. UKvillages.co.uk) as they are corporate (e.g. feedback forums on Shell.com). The most important elements are information, discussion and recommendation:

Information
Community areas of sites have dedicated content for their target customers. For example, motorcycle manufacturer Ducati.com, uses its email newsletter to encourage users to join the 'Ducati community'. Ideally, community content should be user-generated, such as women's portal ivillage.co.uk, which encouraged readers to send in pictures of themselves to appear as models on their home page. Some sites also use 'white paper' or 'best practice' papers as guides to discussion and thought. The idea is to encourage customers to visit, take part and learn. Web tools can also create a stronger tie to a site, such as customised content or home pages (e.g. myYahoo!).

Discussion
Successful community allows users to discuss their topic of interest. This may be as simple as encouraging feedback loops, sharing customer replies to frequently asked questions, or consumer-to-consumer chat such as the popular message boards for BBC soap EastEnders (bbc.co.uk/eastenders). Although there are free chat and messageboard software packages such as multicity.com

corporate software can cost several thousand pounds plus the ongoing costs of someone to moderate the responses.

Recommendation

Recommendations include customer product reviews, ratings or allowing users to email pages or content to friends. Investment site Motley Fool (fool.co.uk) allows users to rate each other's message-board postings and ranks the most popular for other users. Another example is Amazon.co.uk, which asks users to refer a friend to the site, in return for gift certificates.

Adding a community feel to a site requires a thorough understanding of the user base, aided by researching current **newsgroups**, chat rooms and competitors. Community is also a great way to gather research, through data capture and monitoring discussions. Adding a degree of community to a site is difficult, yet with sufficient targeted content, will at least encourage customers to use your site more as a source of information and reference, and not simply as an e-commerce store.

Further information

www.onlinecommunityreport.com (industry news and information)
communities.msn.com (Microsoft community portal)
Community Building on the Web (useful book by Kim)
Mistake 8 – Limited user feedback, *see p. 16*

54 Anti-corporate websites

The Internet allows dissatisfied customers to take their complaints to an international audience, by setting up anti-corporate websites. Sites such as mcspotlight.org (about McDonalds) or noaol.com (about AOL) are simple to set up given the ease of copying branding from official websites and the low cost of web **hosting**. From a small complaint, these sites can quickly grow out of all proportion, encouraging other customers to vent their anger against a company. More recently, anti-corporate viral emails have emerged – Veuve Clicquot was forced to post a notice on its website home page as a result of a hoax email, which promised free champagne from the company if you forwarded the email to friends.

Companies make several mistakes when dealing with such sites. Firstly they do not have a process to monitor when these sites are created. Secondly they tend to be heavy handed by instantly threatening legal action. The problem can be made even worse when the anti-corporate site ranks higher than the official site on search engines. But, by far the worst mistake is that taken by too many companies – failing to take action or ignoring their existence altogether.

The solution

Discovering anti-corporate sites needs to be more than a matter of chance. Your PR department should have a monitoring process in place. It can be easier to outsource monitoring to companies like Cyber Alert who can report back automatically. Many anti-corporate sites are a variation of your official web address (e.g. noamazon.com) so register all negative variations. Companies such as NetNames also offer web-address monitoring and can report whenever an address, which includes your company or brand names, has been registered.

Before you get lawyers involved (and potentially unwanted media attention), try and talk to the site's owner to see if you can resolve their complaints. If the site is spreading untruths then the laws of libel apply online – and a site's service provider can quickly be contacted to close down the site. Given freedom of speech rights, this approach is unlikely to work if the site is hosted in the US. Another approach is to set up a 'pro-company' site. Nike did this with nikebiz.com, which gave information and showed video of its Asian factories, after high-profile claims of poor working conditions. But it can be difficult to maintain integrity with this approach, if you are seen to be too closely involved.

A search-engine strategy is also valuable. Many customers will miss the anti-corporate site if you succeed in pushing your official site to a higher ranking on the key search engines. Yet by far the most effective solution is to improve your online customer feedback. It's amazing how many companies spend thousands in legal fees against anti-corporate sites but have inadequate customer feedback. Some companies such as Dunkin Donuts, have even managed to convert anti-corporate sites into wider customer feedback areas, by providing funding.

One customer complaint can quickly escalate and tarnish your reputation online, so you need to be both aware and able to act swiftly.

Further information

www.cyberalert.com
www.netnames.com
Mistake 83 – No competitive-intelligence strategy, see p. 166
Mistake 35 – Copyright infringement, see p. 70
Mistake 8 – Limited user feedback, see p. 16

55 Poor product information

A major reason why so few online shoppers convert to buyers is that e-commerce sites lack detailed product information. Online, products are two-dimensional, there are no assistants immediately available to answer questions and, if the site is a lesser known brand, shoppers will use product information as an aid to gauging the trustworthiness of the vendor.

Sites that simply transfer their offline product brochures to the web or use basic picture and product descriptions, are not taking advantage of the quick comparative benefits offered by online shopping. The average online shopper visits three or four sites before making a purchase. If product information is poor, they simply go elsewhere to gather what they need. And, when they finally make the decision to buy, they are much less likely to return to the same site to make the purchase.

The solution

Search or surf
Shoppers have different preferences. Some prefer to surf and click their way through product lists, others with a clearer idea of what they want prefer to search. Both options must be available and easily accessible from every page of the site. Site-statistics packages can track surf paths and search terms which provides useful insights into shoppers' behaviour.

Group products
Showing all products of a particular type on one page allows shoppers to make comparisons rather than placing one product per page or listing them alphabetically. Grouping in terms of bundled solutions (e.g. tennis balls with rackets) is widely used in offline stores and facilitates cross-selling.

Offer comparisons
Most shopping-comparison portals compare on price but should also compare on features and benefits. This helps to reassure shoppers that they are making the right decision.

Avoid distractions

As soon as a shopper shows interest in the e-commerce process, all other distractions such as advertising should be minimised, although there should be options to revisit product-information pages without having to restart the process again.

Zoom in on pictures

A study by PriceWaterhouse Coopers in March 2001 showed that for 44 per cent of shoppers, close-up product views increase their likelihood of buying.

Display benefits

Don't just list product features. Showing photographs of products actually being used also has a positive effect.

Show availability

Don't make shoppers wait until checkout to find a product is out of stock.

Clear information

Product details that are hidden, such as behind 'mouse-over' effects, in drop-down lists or that require scrolling should be avoided. For technical product specifications, a glossary can also be useful.

Independent verification

Where possible include customer reviews, press product tests, ratings or manufacturers' awards. There are also a number of sites that allow consumers to rate products such as dooyoo.co.uk.

Further information

Mistake 19 – Abandoned shopping carts, see p. 38
Mistake 16 – Ineffective search, see p. 32

56 The wrong plug-in

Competitive pressures and the desire to offer users rich, engaging content, has given rise to the use of **plug-in** software for Internet **browsers**. However, using plug-ins is a balancing act, given the time and inconvenience to users who need to download them. The main plug-ins are video/audio-based such as RealPlayer or QuickTime; animation or games-based such as **Flash** or Shockwave; document-based such as Acrobat Reader; or application specific such as plug-ins for 360° picture viewers or virtual tours.

Sites either use too many plug-ins or make them integral to a site, thereby alienating many users. This is often made worse by using the very latest version of a plug-in or underestimating how long it will take users to download a plug-in at normal modem speed.

Although there is research, in particular for online shopping, that consumers are keen to use engaging tools (such as virtual tours or 3D chat), there is a significant difference between what consumers would do and what they actually can do given their current system limitations.

The solution

Research user base

You need to estimate how many of your users have the plug-in you wish to use. The table below shows the recent uptake of popular plug-ins. If targeting users at work, they may have faster corporate Internet connections but many companies restrict employees downloading any content from the Internet because of viruses. Also consider users who view your content over other platforms such as web TV, as they do not accept all plug-ins.

Plug-in	Percentage
Quicktime	38
RealPlayer	54
Shockwave	60
Acrobat Reader	67
Windows Media Player	68
Flash	96

Source: Macromedia/NPD Online March 2001. US Survey

Choose the right version

Over 95 per cent of European users have Flash but far fewer have the latest version. Similarly, only approximately half have the 2001 version of Shockwave. Your designers or agency may push you to use the latest version as it allows them to be more creative, but don't let this stop you using earlier versions that will reach more users.

Be honest

You must be upfront about your use of plug-ins in your communications. There's nothing more irritating than responding to a promotion for a website that you cannot use. Furthermore, if users don't have the plug-in, be honest about how long it will really take to download the software.

Provide alternatives

Plug-in content should be optional rather than integral to your site. Sniffer code can be added to detect if users have the plug-in you are using and, if not, presents more basic yet immediately functional content. Sites with Shockwave games also successfully use simple previews that users can view, which encourages them to download the Shockwave plug-in and play the game.

Using plug-ins doesn't mean you have to design to the lowest specification or avoid multimedia content – you just need to take account of their effect on your target audience and ultimately your traffic.

Further information

www.browserwatch.com (regular browser and plug-in news)
www.macromedia.com/software (latest statistics on plug-in penetration)
Mistake 33 – Inappropriate use of Flash, see p. 66

57 Browser hijacking

Browser hijacking was a technique originally used on gambling and adult websites. It removes or disables parts of a user's browser, with the aim of making it more difficult for them to leave. Some mainstream sites have since taken these ideas and applied them to their own site:

Disabled back button

The browser Back button is a key navigational tool but sites can switch it off. Sites that use **Flash** as either an introduction or as navigation can also render the Back button useless and is particularly confusing if used on the home page. Sites have also been known to add a delay to the Back button of a few seconds to prevent leaving the site until the home page has loaded.

Pop-up windows

Pop-up windows are used to display certain types of content, such as **microsites**, search functions or e-commerce shops. Sites delete the toolbar at the top of the browser and, sometimes, the scrollbar from these windows. This removes any navigation and prevents users printing pages or using the Back button. Removing the scrollbar also means that users with monitors set to a low resolution may not see the whole pop-up. Sites that link to others by using full-page pop-up windows sometimes also remove the browser navigation to make it more difficult for users to browse the linked site rather than their own, even though this is the whole point of having links in the first place.

The solution

Browser hijacking occurs for two reasons. One is the misguided belief that making a site more difficult to leave encourages people to stay. The reality is that it confines, confuses and irritates users so that they are encouraged to go elsewhere. The second is that this is seen as a technical issue and left to website designers, when it really should concern sales and marketing.

The Back button should never be disabled (smart users can get around it anyway) and you should not link to other sites that use this technique. Some search engines will refuse to list your site if you do. There are some exceptions, for example, major banks remove browser navigation as a safety measure on secure pages. If linking to another site, either link in the same browser window or open up a new full browser window. Although opening up a second full window used to be frowned upon, it is now more widely accepted. Flash introductions to websites should also be avoided because they disable the Back button amongst other problems.

Most managers are unlikely to be aware of browser hijacking until it is brought to their attention or may not see its importance. But it is equivalent to letting customers into a store and locking the door behind them. It wouldn't be tolerated offline and shouldn't be tolerated online either.

58 | Animation over information

As tools to create online animation, such as **Flash** and **dHTML** have developed, the use of animation in web and advertising creatives has become widespread.

Although animation is ideal for gaining and maintaining attention, it doesn't necessarily make a site or advertisement more effective and its interruption-based approach can irritate users. It should be the message, offer or brand that in itself encourages click through. With the development of faster **broadband** connections, there is the temptation to use more animation just because bandwidth allows.

The key to using animation on the Internet is understanding how it adds value, its limitations and when not to use it.

The solution

Animation should support user goals, rather than hinder them. For example, the fully animated version of e4.com helped broadcaster Channel 4 brand 'E4', their new entertainment channel.

Does the animation add value? A rotating logo doesn't make the sales process any easier or tell you anything more about the brand. If animation does not add value then it is just taking up page file size and increasing page download time. Consider other ways to create emphasis. Good use of colour, shape, scale and contrast can all hold attention as well as animation.

Limit rotations. There is a tendency to create endless animation loops on the Internet. This is especially true with banner advertisements. dHTML banners, which allow animations to come out of the banner into the page content, are very annoying if they loop continuously. There is also evidence to suggest that users block out anything that loops, thinking it is advertising. Some sites have policies of limiting rotations – Yahoo!, for example, will only accept banners with one rotation. On certain pages, timing for banners is also important. As a general rule, a banner animation over 5–6 seconds will test users' patience.

Notify users in advance if an animation will take time to download with standard modem connections or requires **plug-ins**, then offer alternative content to users that do not want to wait. In the case of e4.com the site defaults to a basic version but gives users with the appropriate plug-ins the choice of a 'full-on' animated experience.

Animation applies beyond web-page design to **HTML** emails and other devices such as handheld PCs and **WAP**. These platforms have greater design restrictions, e.g. some interactive TV banners are static due to technical limitations.

As campaigns develop across platforms with more restrictive technologies, designers and marketers are now being forced to look again at animation – and rely more on the message and creativity to improve effectiveness.

Further information

www.animation.about.com (comprehensive guide to animation)
Effective Web Animation (useful book by Hamlin)
Mistake 33 – Inappropriate use of Flash, see *p. 66*
Mistake 30 – Splash pages, see *p. 60*

59 Pricing errors

It's easy to make clerical errors but, on the Internet, several companies have already discovered that simple pricing errors potentially risk huge losses.

One of the earliest UK cases was back in 1999 with retailer Argos.co.uk, which accidentally priced a television set at £2.99, rather than £299. Within a short space of time, it had received an estimated £1 million worth of orders, including one for 1700 sets. The result was threatened legal action and negative public relations.

Most of the online pricing errors so far have been due to human mistakes, software errors, or accidental loading of data from test to live sites. Nonetheless, companies need to realise the consequences of simple errors online if they want to avoid costly and embarrassing mistakes

The solution

Companies have to accept that human error can occur and set procedures in place accordingly. E-commerce reporting software needs to include alerts that signal if a product is experiencing abnormal sale patterns. A sudden rise in orders per customer might indicate a pricing error.

You also need to make a decision on whether to honour your mistake, which will be determined by cost of orders versus the cost of negative public relations. Whereas Argos, understandably, didn't want to honour £1 million worth of orders, supermarket Tesco.com did offer to honour a price discrepancy of £63 for a boxed DVD set it priced incorrectly. The alternative is not to honour the price but to provide a special offer in return. When Compaq Computer accidentally priced a handheld PC at £1 instead of £530, they offered buyers a free printer if they paid the correct price.

Although it is not legally clear, Argos successfully argued before their case went to court that their site was not an offer to sell but rather an 'invitation to treat'. Your site terms and conditions should therefore include a disclaimer clause to cover this eventuality; namely that a contract is not formed until a separate confirmation of sale is sent to the customer.

Another option, which needs careful management, is price testing. In September 2000, Amazon.com issued a formal apology for price testing that resulted in customers being offered random discounts of between 20 and

40 per cent for the same DVD. Such live market testing can easily alienate customers.

Unlike offline pricing, the real problem is not the mistake but the speed at which it is communicated online. Although it may be unrealistic for a customer to expect a product at a ridiculous price, companies must be prepared to manage their expectations and the press if they want to minimise the damage to their corporate reputation.

Further information

Mistake 45 – Lower online prices, see p. 90

60 Advertising on small sites

Websites generally make revenue from e-commerce, advertising or a mixture of the two. With Internet advertising expected to be the fastest growing sector of the media industry, it would be easy to imagine that adding banner or other forms of advertising to a site will generate significant income. But this has mainly been the case for large, high-traffic sites rather than small to medium-sized businesses.

If a smaller site wants to host advertising, they have a choice of either running it in-house, which tends to be too costly, or outsourcing to an advertising network. Networks represent hundreds of individual sites that do not have the resources to manage their own in-house sales team. In principle this sounds ideal but for small sites creates several problems.

There are a limited number of networks, the major ones including Double Click, Engage and 24/7 Media, but they will not accept sites with low-traffic volumes. Double Click, for example, rejects sites serving under 1 million **page impressions** a month, whilst 24/7 Media prefers 750,000 impressions a month although will consider less. All networks charge a commission, which can range from 30 per cent to 50 per cent. For small sites, this means that the revenue generated is usually hardly worth the effort. For example, if a site serves 20,000 impressions a month and the network sells them to an advertiser at a price of £25 per 1000 banner impressions, this generates just £250 for the site (after the network takes its 50 per cent commission).

There are alternatives to both in-house sales or network advertising which should be considered, as sites with less than 100,000 impressions a month will find advertising a revenue stream that is difficult to sustain.

The solution

There are a number of advertising networks that will represent sites with lower traffic levels. ValueClick, for example, accepts sites with tens of thousands of page impressions and they also pay on a cost-per-click basis rather than on cost-per-banner served. When approaching these networks, be clear on the payment methods and, in particular, their **server** reliability. If they fail to serve an advert to your site this can return an error page to the user, which looks as if your site is unavailable. Some of the larger networks will also consider a site with low traffic if it targets a specific niche demographic.

For niche sites, the low revenue generated from networks means that selling in-house may be the only option. Rather than trying to sell thousands of banner adverts the best approach is to sell packaged sponsorship deals. These tend to be better value and the site can charge more as the package is not based on a set cost per thousand. For example, teenage site pupiline.net signed a sponsorship deal with Burger King to promote part-time job applications in local restaurants. There are other revenue opportunities small sites can target, such as banner exchanges (which are best avoided) and affiliate programmes (which also do not guarantee significant income).

If a small site isn't based on e-commerce or is too broad to offer niche sponsorship then advertising revenue is unlikely to solve the problem and the site will need to question its existence or redevelop to survive.

Further information

www.doubleclick.com
www.engage.com
www.valueclick.com
www.247europe.com
Mistake 72 – Excluding sponsorship, see p. 144

61 Frames

The mistake   Design   Marketing   Strategy

Web designers have long disapproved of the use of frames in page design. They are a feature that can split up a page into separate areas, often three – the navigation bar usually on the left, the title area with company logo at the top and the main page content. Frames therefore allow the navigation to remain constant whilst the main page scrolls.

Many early sites made poor use of frames and although they are less common now, poor application still produces numerous problems:

Screen resolutions
More sites are optimising their pages for higher screen resolutions. But, if users with low resolution view such pages, the frames become too big for the screen and 'scroll bars' appear alongside, reducing the site's appeal.

Bookmarks and links
If a framed page is **bookmarked** or linked-to directly via the web address rather than the home page, only that frame will show, ignoring the other navigation or title frames.

Search engines
Have great difficulty referencing framed pages, ensuring your site gets a very poor ranking. Again, if a page is found, the surrounding frames will not be displayed.

Use of frames is subjective as, if applied properly, they have the advantage of providing consistent navigation and make sites easier to update. The problem is that small or low-budget sites are still making fundamental mistakes in their application.

The solution

Frames, if used carefully and sparingly, can appear invisible to the untrained eye. Whether to use them will depend on the navigation needs of your site, the target audience, the budget and the importance of search engines in your marketing strategy.

If they are used, precise coding by your designers can help eliminate some of the problems. Framed pages also can be difficult to print, so adding a 'print page' option to your site should be considered. The most prolific use of frames at present, is at the top of a page, when linking out to other sites and has been used by major portals such as MSN.co.uk. If you do use this approach, keep the frame as small as possible and ensure the page you link to doesn't look as if it is still part of your site, as this can have legal implications. If search engineering is important it is best not to use frames on your home page. Secure pages should also avoid frames as they will take longer to download.

The many disadvantages of frames on the whole outweigh the benefits, especially if they adversely affect search-engine and linking capabilities. You won't find frames on most successful high-volume sites. So it is in management's interest to take a look at whether their site uses frames, rather than leaving it solely to their designers' discretion.

Further information

www.htmlhelp.com
www.websitetips.com
(for both sites search on 'frames' for a range of useful articles)
Mistake 77 – Deep linking, *see p. 154*

62 Not auditing your website

Every corporate website measures its site traffic and makes available the results, generally in terms of **page impressions, unique visitors** or registered users. Site statistics are not only a measure of success but also affect advertising rates and the company's stock price and value. Yet how can other companies gauge the accuracy of internally produced data? For example, in February 2001, publicly listed company E-District had its CEO and shares suspended, after allegedly overstating revenue and traffic figures. This occurred because the London Stock Exchange did not require them to audit non-financial metrics.

> Over one in three senior marketers express unease about Internet accountability. 86 per cent agree that third-party Internet audits are crucial to the buying decision.
>
> *Source*: Marketing Forum UK, 2000

Third-party audits have long been a tradition with offline, in particular print media. However, it is only larger sites that are willing to invest in online audits. For the majority of small to medium-sized sites, the cost of auditing is seen to be prohibitive. Yet in an industry with many, similar competing websites, advertisers look to auditing as an aid to choosing sites and in particular, ensuring accountability.

The solution

Log-file based

The traditional online audit is based on analysing the server **log files** generated every time a user visits your site. Companies such as the Audit Bureau of Circulation (ABC) offer this service. They audit the process by which you produce your statistics rather than looking at every single piece of data. You do not need an audit every month as you can become 'certified' with just one month's audit, although regular certification is preferable. The cost depends on your size, but can be over £5000 per month for large sites. As well as your page impressions or visitor numbers, **streaming** media content (e.g. video or live webcasts) can also be audited.

The Internet Advertising Bureau (IAB) develops guidelines for online auditing to give 'powerful independent verification'. These recommend a quarterly audit (or twice yearly as a minimum); cover at least the home page; cover a standard calendar month to help with cross-site comparisons and be completed by a recognised third-party auditor.

Browser based

Audit processes such as from the company Red Sherrif, measure your site statistics based on browser usage rather than log files. This is said to be more accurate as log files under report traffic due to **cached pages** or corporate **firewalls**. The result can significantly increase your reported statistics. However, the process can cost thousands of pounds a month, and you will still need to pay if you also want separate audit certification from a company like ABC.

In an increasingly unstable industry, every company needs to engender trust with both advertisers and shareholders – auditing can be a worthwhile investment in achieving this.

Further information

www.abce.org.uk (ABC Electronic)
www.iabuk.net (IAB)
www.redsherrif.com
Mistake 7 – Not measuring website ROI, see p. 14

63 Ineffective viral marketing

The mistake   Design **Marketing** Strategy

Viral marketing has been a buzzword since the late 1990s, whereby consumers pass on commercial messages by emailing them to friends. Executives with limited budgets jump at the chance to try viral marketing as it can be very cost-effective.

With so many companies testing viral marketing, consumers have been interrupted with too many poor quality, badly targeted campaigns. Viral marketing is more than adding a 'send to a friend' function to your website. The technique was seen as 'uncommercial', but is now becoming mainstream, with brands like Nike and Budweiser using it. This is switching off those marketing-averse consumers originally attracted to the idea.

> Only 13 per cent of Internet users pass on emails from companies. They are worried that they will receive more commercial emails as a result.
>
> *Source*: Lowe Live/BMRB International, January 2001

Furthermore there is debate as to how effective virals are and if they generate real future sales and revenue – rather than just being a public relations gimmick. With the average office worker getting over forty emails a day, a successful viral campaign now needs a lot of thought.

The solution

For consumers to pass on and endorse your message, it must have value to them. There are four types of value: entertainment/amusement, games, offers and social/charity. You have to be careful of needing **plug-ins** for games, which can make them difficult to play. Offers do not have to offer something for free – the Lowe Live/BMRB research showed that the promise of a reward was only half as motivating as informative or humorous content in order to pass on an email.

Brand is important. It's easier to pass on an email from a trusted brand, although if the message is seen to be too corporate, the incentive to pass on diminishes. A way around this is to use viral marketing for product launches. Key customers can be offered sneak previews of products or advertising, usually reserved for the press.

Your initial contacts for the campaign need to be well-targeted for the message to be of value. Consider also corporate **firewalls**, which might prevent you sending email attachments. Simple text virals with strong value can, therefore, be more effective.

You also have to be realistic about what you will get back. Despite the difficulty of measuring the results, email databases are the obvious benefit, as is branding. Virals that result in online sales, however, are more likely with impulse purchases or low-value consumables.

The future of viral marketing looks set to spread to a wider audience yet, for that very reason, you will need to work a lot harder to make them effective.

Further information

www.revolution.haynet.com

www.clickz.com

(for both sites search on 'viral marketing' for a range of articles)

Mistake 99 – Advertising in newsgroups and chat rooms, see p. 198

64 No contingency planning

When an online company has to deal with a major disaster it usually relates to a technical problem, corporate/media problem or a combination of the two. On the technical side, a bank might have a web security breach; a retailer might be subject to hacking or a site **outage**. On the corporate side, a car manufacturer may require a product recall or to announce major job losses.

Too often, online procedures to deal with these problems are not planned in advance. If a site has an outage, for a few hours or more, management will often just put the site back up and hope no one notices. If a negative press story breaks, companies often avoid mentioning it on their website, even though this is the first place consumers and the press will look.

With an increasing amount of online operations outsourced (such as web **hosting** or e-commerce management) there is a greater risk that something will go wrong and, too often, management don't do anything about it until it is too late.

The solution

In the case of technical problems a disaster recovery plan needs to be set up. This involves identifying all possible risks, prioritising them, training resource and setting-up procedures. It need not be complex. For some firms it may be as simple as ensuring they have a standard dial-up PC for updating the website, if their corporate network fails. For others it may mean ensuring the call centre is informed every time the website fails.

In the case of media disasters, constantly updating the website should have a high priority. Major airlines realise this, and have a simple system that replaces the entire website with an information page in the case of a major incident. Staff responsible for updating this page are given content management tools and training so they can update the site themselves. **Server** capacities should also be scalable in these circumstances, otherwise any spike in traffic to the website can cause it to slow or crash. Using the website to manage information not only frees resource for other jobs, but presents the company as honest rather than with something to hide.

Another contingency is insurance. Standard product or public-liability insurance does not safeguard sites against e-commerce disasters; so more insurance companies are offering cyber-liability cover. This can protect against lost revenue and the cost of repairing systems or data if a site has been hacked. But it can be expensive given the difficulty in evaluating acceptable risk.

Contingency plans are necessary for small e-commerce sites just as much as major corporations, as all disasters can result in lost revenue. As the Internet user matures, they are less prepared to accept technical errors or mishandling of online media and companies will be increasingly judged on the accuracy and speed of their response.

Further information

www.abi.org.uk (Association of British Insurers)
Mistake 68 – Lack of load testing, see p. 136
Mistake 26 – Poor quality PR, see p. 52

65 Over-use of banners

The mistake   Design   **Marketing**   Strategy

Banner advertisements are synonymous with online advertising. This is given that they are easy to understand and cost-effective to produce. They are also cost-effective to buy and easy to use in contra deals. However, banner **click through rates** have fallen dramatically, to an average below 0.5 per cent and banner advertising's share of the online advertising market is expected to fall over the next five years. Nonetheless, they are still the most widely used form of online advertising.

Other forms of online advertising are less attractive due to higher media and production costs and a lack of understanding of the alternatives. Unless a campaign is solely branding, marketers can no longer rely on standard banners alone to generate response and need to consider all the alternatives if they want their campaigns to be both richer and more effective.

The solution

Pop-ups
Almost as well-recognised as banners, pop-ups are small windows that appear above the main **browser** window and are often disliked by users for their intrusive approach. They can be of slightly greater file size than banners and higher click-through rates can be as a result of users trying to close them down. When buying media space, they can cost over 2½ times the price of banners.

Superstitials
Look just like **pop-ups** but download in the background when a user isn't browsing. This allows them to be up to 100K in file size (compared to 10–12K for banners) and allows for larger, rich-media, audio-visual creatives or data capture. They can produce double-digit response rates but you will pay a premium for the production and media space.

Interstitials
Similar in look and cost to superstitials, interstitials appear briefly between pages, almost like a commercial break. They are particularly intrusive to the user experience but can be used for short branding campaigns.

dHTML banners

'Dynamic' HTML adverts often look like banners but allow the creative to come out of the banner and float across the web page. They have to be carefully targeted to avoid annoying users and the cost of production will be significantly higher than other forms of online advertising.

Flash banners

Macromedia **Flash** software creates better animated and engaging creative. It also produces higher responses and if users don't have the Flash **plug-in**, this can be detected and a standard banner served instead.

Other forms

The Internet Advertising Bureau has developed a range of new advertising formats. These include the Skyscraper, which is a long banner that runs the vertical length of a page, and Rectangles, which are box-shaped.

The important point to note about all these alternatives to banners are that the higher response rates may well be as a result of novelty or intrusion on the user experience. They are really only options for those with five-figure budgets, and companies with less should consider the use of search engineering, email advertising or sponsorship as well as banners, for more cost-effective approaches.

Poor creative and media targeting will produce poor results no matter which option you can afford. But, overall, online advertising must be integrated into other forms of on and offline marketing, as concentrating predominantly on banners is really no longer a viable option.

Further information

www.iabuk.net (Internet Advertising Bureau)
www.tangozebra.com (solutions provider for interactive online advertising)
Mistake 15 – Intrusive online advertising, see p. 30

66 Video streaming quality

On average, 10 per cent of online companies offer some form of video content on their sites and, although this is an attempt to add interactive and compelling content, the reality rarely meets anything near broadcast-like quality. The result is small-sized video that is slow to download, jerky, broken and dependent on **plug-ins**.

> A regular quality index of the top twenty streaming media websites, only gives an average score of 2/10 (where 10 is near DVD quality). MTV Interactive is one of the few sites that regularly scores the highest at over 4.0.
>
> *Source*: Keynote Streaming Index, Feb–June 2001

The main problem is that users do not have the bandwidth with which to view video to a reasonable quality. **Broadband** access will change this; already those with broadband are 50 per cent more likely to access **streaming** content than those with narrowband access. But broadband is not expected to reach more than a quarter of European homes by 2005. Companies need to add video content to their sites with care if they want it to at least meet basic user expectations.

The solution

Audio
The quality of streaming audio is generally better online so can be substituted for video where possible, although not every user has sound, especially those at work.

Length and version
Keep video clips short and tell users in advance the size of the file and its running time. Minimising the movement in video recordings will also improve viewing quality. Ideally you should create several different versions of each clip for different user bandwidths/Internet speeds.

Player

You should also consider creating different versions for the different user-video plug-ins. Windows Media Player is the most popular, closely followed by RealPlayer.

Audience

The need for high quality video depends on your audience. For example, content is more important than quality for a business-to-business conference site than an entertainment site.

Download

You should also consider offering downloads of video content rather than streaming, which gives users greater control over viewing, although gives them an online copy which might have copyright implications.

Server

Web **servers** weren't designed to handle video streaming efficiently. A standard server will probably handle about a thousand simultaneous user streams so you will need to invest in specialist servers such as RealSystem iQ if you expect a larger audience. If you use an external web host you should also agree minimum streaming guarantees in your contract.

Until faster Internet access becomes widespread, sites need to question the true value of video content. As pay-per-view and pay-per-download revenue models are introduced, users will no longer tolerate sub-standard quality.

Further information

www.realnetworks.com
www.keynote.com
www.streamingmediaworld.com
www.streamingmedia.com
Mistake 68 – Lack of load testing, see p. 136
Mistake 56 – The wrong plug-in, see p. 112

67 Online advertising does not build brands

The mistake   Design **Marketing** Strategy

One of the main benefits of online advertising is its measurability. But with declining banner **click through rates** and the need to improve targeting, marketers are focusing too much on click through as a measure of success. Online advertising is seen more as a direct response mechanism as sites turn to traditional offline media for branding.

> Only 15 per cent of online advertising campaigns are measured on how effectively they extend a brand.
>
> *Source:* Jupiter Media Metrix Inc, June 2001

The focus on direct response is partly due to the instant results and nature of the Internet, whereas branding is only effective over time. Branding is more than advertising and encompasses the values, emotions and functions of an Internet offering, but this gives online advertising an ideal opportunity to build brand awareness and affect post-campaign recall and purchase decisions.

The solution

Users who see banners can be affected even if they are not prompted to click. Research has shown that users can return to a site up to thirty days after seeing a banner, which indicates a level of brand awareness. Advertising networks can measure this affect by serving a **cookie** to users who receive the banner and recognising it if they ever subsequently return to the advertiser's site. This has implications for banner design. As well as being able to put across brand values or messages, they need to be simple, clear and make the logo or web address visible to aid later recall. Adding urgency to the call to action can also assist.

Research by Dynamic Logic and 24/7 Media (October 2000) showed that banner advertising increases brand awareness by 7 per cent, advertising recall by 27 per cent and message association by 20 per cent. It also found that design elements such as larger logos and banners, the use of human faces and reducing design clutter can all improve the effect on branding. Dynamic Logic's research has also demonstrated that increased frequency of viewing an online advert improves brand awareness. In the case of a campaign by Travelocity.com, four viewings increased awareness by 44 per cent. This is the opposite to **click through rates** which generally decline with increased viewing frequency.

Beyond banners, more interactive **pop-ups** such as **superstitials** allow for richer, more interactive creatives which engage consumers although, equally, have the potential to annoy. Sponsorship is also increasingly popular as a long-term alternative to banners.

Online advertising works best when integrated with offline media as it reinforces the online creative. However, a report in 2001 by Morgan Stanley Dean Witter concluded that Internet banners can have higher brand recall than TV or print, although this works better for established rather than developing brands.

Like offline advertising, measuring the effects of online branding is more difficult than click through but this doesn't mean that it should be ignored. Branding is a lot more than advertising and no matter how effective online media is at generating awareness and intent, it is the site the adverts click through to that needs to work the hardest at converting the initial awareness into a full brand proposition.

Further information

www.dynamiclogic.com
www.iabuk.net (Internet Advertising Bureau)
Mistake 50 – Damaging brand reputation, see p. 100
Mistake 24 – Measuring advertising by click-through, see p. 48

68 Lack of load testing

It's too easy to think that marketing a website is more about the message than backend operations. But too many companies are finding that taking their website for granted results in sites that are slow or crash as promotions produce unmanageable spikes in traffic. The result is lost revenue, damaged reputation and can create surges in other business areas, such as call centres.

In 2000 demand to place orders on Sony's website for its new PlayStation2 console, caused it to crash for two hours. The following month, demand was so great for the first e-book from author Stephen King, that his site also crashed, just hours after going online.

If a site does prepare by testing maximum user loads in advance it is usually done the wrong way round. A promotion is planned and **servers** are then checked to see if they can handle the anticipated load, rather than building the promotion around what the server can handle in the first place.

Gartner Group estimate that people and operational processes contribute to 80 per cent of site failures, so revise your internal procedures to minimise the risks.

The solution

Load testing to estimate the maximum number of concurrent users should form part of a wider disaster-recovery plan, to cope when too much traffic crashes your site. This involves regular performance analysis and back-up servers. Comdisco estimates that a third of websites do not have a back-up recovery plan. Many managers still think of disaster in terms of fires or floods rather than viruses, hackers or traffic peaks.

Performance analysis can be cost effective for smaller sites using software such as Astra Site Manager which reports on a range of problems including load. Software such as Watchfire's Macrobot is excellent at testing your site based on 'scenarios', be that general browsing or making a purchase. For larger companies, testing needs to be outsourced to specialists such as Comdisco or IBM Business Recovery.

A disaster-recovery plan should also include back-up **servers** if traffic crashes your site. Either with 'warm recovery' which will return your site within a few hours or 'hot recovery' which switches immediately to the back-up server if the site goes down. The latter option is preferable but more expensive.

Predicting traffic is difficult, given the lack of historical data with which many companies have to make decisions. Staggering the rollout of an online promotion will help spread the impact. However, a promotion can affect all areas of your organisation. The key is to ensure that the marketing and technical sides of your business work together from the start.

Further information

www.watchfire.com
www.comdisco.com
www.brs.ibm.com
Mistake 64 – No contingency planning, *see p. 128*

69 Ineffective loyalty schemes

The mistake   Design   **Marketing**   Strategy

There has been much debate over offline loyalty schemes, particularly in the supermarket industry. Some see loyalty cards as an integral part of their strategy, whilst others such as Asda and Safeway have dropped them in favour of lower prices. Now that such schemes are available online, the same question arises – are they more than data-collection exercises, and do they actually work?

> Only 28 per cent of Internet users have heard of online reward schemes, and only 10 per cent have participated. Price is seen as the main reason for repeat visits.
>
> *Source*: Customer Report/MORI, March 2001

Site owners have a choice: migrate any existing scheme online, join a programme such as www.ipoints.co.uk, or create your own. Online loyalty is more fragile than offline given the ease at which customers can click elsewhere, especially if the scheme only concentrates on discounts or money-off vouchers which can easily be copied by competitors. And similar to offline schemes there is evidence that customers are members of up to three programmes, which doesn't indicate that they are particularly loyal.

The solution

Whether you join an online programme or create your own, no matter how basic, you need to choose a scheme that is simple – e.g. the success of airline frequent-flyer programmes rests on their simplicity, miles = free flights. Simplicity is also important, as one of the main problems with online loyalty schemes is promotion and awareness.

Unlike other online marketing, loyalty schemes will not produce instant returns. Different customers, both new and those experienced to the net, will be prepared to involve themselves to differing degrees. You should recognise and reflect this in the rewards you offer. And, just like offline programmes, you have to encourage a redemption within the first six–eight months if you want to create a longer-term relationship. The holy grail of online loyalty is personalisation and speed of response. High levels of targeted communications will in themselves engender loyalty rather than special offers.

Yet, above all, an effective loyalty scheme needs to backed up with effective and consistent functionality. 50 per cent discounts mean nothing if you fail to meet basic customer-service or site-navigation expectations and this is where most sites and the schemes they run fall down.

Online loyalty schemes on their own won't guarantee loyalty and for many sites, investing in the basics of better site design and customer service, will do more for repeat custom, than discount or third-party programmes.

70 Not reacting to site abandonment

The mistake   Design   Marketing   **Strategy**

Visitors to websites will leave prematurely when a site does not live up to expectation. It is estimated that up to 50 per cent of sites are abandoned due to slow-loading pages and over two-thirds during the e-commerce process. Whether they are abandoning shopping carts or unsubscribing from services, e-commerce companies are focusing too much resource on customer acquisition rather than retention.

The importance of database size rather than quality is clear in how site performance is measured, in terms of total traffic rather than the percentage who return. Customer abandonment occurs a lot more easily and quickly online. Companies shouldn't just accept the cost of this, and need to be more active in winning back their customers.

The solution

E-commerce process
Up to three-quarters of online shopping carts are abandoned. Rather than accepting this fact, if abandonment is after the point of collecting personal data, you can email customers with an incentive to return and complete their transaction.

Unsubscribe
If customers unsubscribe from an e-newsletter or service, use the opportunity to ask why they are unsubscribing. Even if they still unsubscribe, a confirmation email can be used as a last attempt to offer incentives to register for other related services.

Site statistics
All good site-statistics packages will show you from which pages customers are leaving your site. This can show trends, which can be used to place promotions on key pages to encourage them to stay longer.

Promote feedback
If customers have a problem, then clear contact channels give them a choice between feedback or site abandonment. If you don't promote feedback then they will have no other choice but to leave.

Abandonment pop-ups

Pop-up advertising can also be served to users as they leave a site. If they leave from key pages such as e-commerce, this technique could be used to ask why they are leaving, but would need to be managed to avoid irritation.

Competitor abandonment

You can take advantage of customers who enter your site direct from a competitor. By recognising this, you can serve targeted content or promotions to take advantage of their defection.

With all these processes, you need to give customers a measure of value (even a crude measure based on past purchases alone) to determine who is worth chasing, although some processes are cost effective enough to apply to everyone. It is also wise to offer alternatives when contacting defectors. Offering to complete an abandoned shopping cart by phone will have a greater affect than sending customers back to the website where the same problems may again arise. Similarly, those unsubscribing from email services could be offered less frequent or offline brochure communications instead.

Retention is not the same as loyalty but it will help to create it. Yet perhaps the quickest way to avoid abandonment, is to better manage site design, service and expectations, so customers don't leave in the first place.

Further information

Customer Winback (book of ideas and case studies by Lowenstein)
Mistake 19 – Abandoned shopping carts, see *p. 38*

71 | First-mover advantage

Conventional new-media wisdom states that for an e-business to be successful it must be first to market. First movers are expected to gain a lead on market share, customer base, distribution channels and proprietary knowledge.

Despite the recent demise of many dot coms, this principle still survives, particularly if you look at the number of companies claiming to be 'first' with a new product or venture. However, although many market leaders were first, it doesn't follow that all those first to market will therefore be leaders.

The principles of first-mover advantage, which may apply offline, are more difficult to replicate online given low barriers to entry, lack of regulation, imitation and the ease by which customers can switch. As a result, more and more companies are discovering that first-mover advantage is a myth and that the benefit is only temporary.

The solution

Certain products lend themselves better to first-mover advantage than others. It is no surprise that retailers selling low-value and easily defined products such as books and CDs have gained greater market share than those selling lifestyle-based products such as clothing, where brand recognition is more important.

The problem with being an innovator is that to remain a leader you have to keep on innovating. It is programmes such as affiliates and 'one-click' shopping that have secured Amazon's success, not that they were initially first to market. However, research and innovation in an uncertain market is costly, especially if it changes unexpectedly, and competitors can benefit from your experience. Furthermore, the rush to be first leads to oversights in other backend operations, like customer service and fulfilment, which can quickly erode any advantage.

There are many examples of companies and products, second or third into a market, that have subsequently dominated, such as AOL or Microsoft's Internet Explorer and Hotmail. It is difficult to sustain momentum, and there are a thousand practical and management issues that can go wrong. Many start-ups have already realised that the barriers to running a successful business are higher than actually entering it. Strategic alliances are an option, such as with lastminute.com and thomascook.com – one benefiting from their first-mover expertise, the other from their brand and distribution network.

It's increasingly difficult to gain first-mover advantage in a global and volatile industry. In the US, the race is no longer first to market but first to patent. Basing your online offering on imitating market leaders might not sound very exciting and won't win column inches in the press – but if you don't have the resource to constantly innovate, it might be the most financially sound strategy you can take.

72 Excluding sponsorship

The mistake   Design **Marketing** Strategy

When marketers consider online advertising, they think banners, **pop-ups** and email. With the trade press constantly extolling the virtues of new interactive forms of advertising such as **superstitials**, it is no surprise that sponsorship opportunities are not fully explored. Sponsorship is not a new concept online but it is a growth market.

Turning to **pop-up** advertising in the light of declining banner **click-through rates** is addressing the problem with greater interruption which encourages users to click elsewhere, whereas good sponsorship or content as marketing produces an integrated and subtler campaign. Sponsorship also bypasses users' sifting out advertising, either subconsciously or with filtering software.

The solution

Brand synergy

Sponsorship allows you to reach a wide audience yet at the same time talk to each user individually. However, the site you sponsor, its environment and demographics must fit with your brand values, otherwise users will see the sponsorship as purely commercial rather than enhancing their experience. Objectives will help determine the right fit – do you want increased traffic, customer/survey data or brand awareness? If you do not want to approach partners yourself, agencies such as Sponsorship Online can act as intermediaries although you may then have to manage a three-way relationship.

Create a dialogue

Effective sponsorship is more than adding a logo. The Internet is the ideal place to let consumers interact with your brand, a technique used successfully by virginradio.co.uk which uses its radio channel to drive listeners to sponsored online **microsites**. Dialogue cannot be achieved instantly and works better if integrated with any offline marketing activity.

Content specifics

Sponsorship can be interpreted in many ways but is often packaged with banners and, increasingly, other platforms such as interactive TV or wireless devices. This approach requires a long-term commitment, deals over three months being increasingly common. Choose a partner who can tailor the package to your needs (e.g. with a bespoke microsite) and provide regular feedback. The price can be subjective. As well as market conditions, expect **page impressions**, agreement length and any exclusivity to be influencing factors.

Sponsorship should not be solely the territory of large brands or high-traffic sites – small companies can benefit from targeting niche sites. Now is also the ideal time to test sponsorship, as more and more media owners offer cost-effective packages, to counteract falling online advertising revenues.

Further information

www.sponsorshiponline.com
www.sports-sponsorship.co.uk (Institute of Sports Sponsorship)

73 Ineffective affiliate marketing

First implemented by Amazon.com, an affiliate programme allows website owners to advertise links and products from another e-commerce site. If the links generate traffic or sales then the site owner earns a commission.

However, most websites who try affiliate programmes discover that they rarely generate significant revenue. The average site will have tried up to five affiliates in an attempt to maximise commission but this provides an inconsistent message to users about site partners. There's also a tendency to opt for the programme with the highest commission, regardless of brand fit.

More companies are offering affiliate programmes as a targeted alternative to online advertising. Site owners need to choose any programme with care if it is to generate revenue rather than taking up valuable real estate on their pages.

The solution

Brand fit
The most important factor is choosing a programme that complements your brand rather than being a bolt-on feature. Aim for one or two long-term affiliate merchants that users will trust. Your traffic also determines fit, e.g. low-traffic sites will not generate much revenue with programmes for low-value products.

Payment
Commission will be based on how many clicks, sales leads, registrations or actual sales your site generates. A click-based scheme will only pay a few pence per click, whereas higher-value products generally offer anything between 5 and 15 per cent commission.

Display
Merchants' products should be integrated into your site's content to improve response and to avoid looking like an advert. Some offer **pop-up** 'microshops', allowing users to visit their store without leaving your site. Some merchants (such as peoplesound.com) also offer other free editorial content, which helps integrate the affiliate shop with the rest of the site.

Advertising

Be sure the page space taken by the programme could not be better sold as advertising, especially as the affiliate merchant gets free branding for every user that does not click.

Time period

Be clear as to whether your commission is paid only if a referral buys in that user session, such as with Amazon's Associates Program. If they return at a later date, you lose out. Some programmes offer up to 90-day post-click time periods to purchase.

Reporting and marketing

Look for programmes that offer regular reports on your performance (ideally with access to real-time software) and marketing support, such as targeted banners which you can download and run on your own site.

Affiliate merchants can be approached directly but more are outsourcing the process to networks such as ukaffiliates.com or commissionjunction.com. But perhaps the most profitable solution is to set up a programme yourself. Software such as AffiliateShop or the Affiliate Tracking Network, can easily be installed. Alternatively all networks sign up new merchants, if you are prepared to pay a set-up and per-transaction fee.

Further information

www.affiliateshop.com
www.affiliatetracking.com
www.affiliatemarketing.co.uk (online affiliate guide)

74 Choosing the wrong web-design agency

Choosing the wrong web-design agency can be a costly mistake, especially with hundreds of agencies in the UK alone to choose from. Creating a list from which to hold a pitch is relatively easy if you have six or seven-figure budgets, but the choice is difficult for small to medium-sized enterprises, especially with no prior recommendation.

Selection is more than just picking names out of the trade press or agencies that advertise their services. A methodical approach is required, especially if you are looking for skills across numerous new media platforms.

The solution

Use this 15-point checklist to select the right agency for you:

1. Projects – split your online projects into four clear areas: website, database/email communications, advertising/**microsites**, and other platform development (e.g. mobile, handheld).
2. Resource – before you start, decide exactly which of these areas you can run internally (with training or new resource, if necessary) and which require specialist external help.
3. Objectives – determine your objectives for each project, ideally as part of a full written brief.
4. Budget – determine your budget, because small budget clients may well get poorer service in large agencies with 'more important' clients.
5. Style – what do you want out of the relationship? Smaller agencies tend to be quicker and more creative whereas larger, cross-media agencies have greater expertise but can be more conservative.
6. List – create your list of potentials, although with a blank sheet this can be quite difficult. The trade-press sites such as Revolution have regular updates on agency activity. Online directories such as the UK Web Design Directory are also a good starting point for smaller agencies outside London. Alternatively, source the agencies that have already designed excellent sites in your industry.
7. Portfolio – for each agency check their full portfolio. Is their previous work in line with your brand values? This is by far the most important requirement. Your Internet offering should be an integral part of your brand,

not an extension of the agency's own portfolio or award list. Portfolios should also include experience of your required functionality (e.g. e-commerce, wireless applications).

8 Testimonials – insist on client testimonials.

9 Maintenance – who will regularly maintain the site? What is the hourly rate or can the agency create content management systems with which to implement changes?

10 Added value – what additional services does the agency offer (marketing, sales, **hosting**, etc.) and at what cost?

11 Service – determine the standard design-process and service-level agreements, e.g. how many creatives will you get per brief, does this include amends, are there penalty clauses?

12 Partners – no matter what they claim, most agencies outsource some work to strategic partners. Make sure you find out who these are.

13 Account team – how many dedicated people will work on your account?

14 Integration – if you're looking for several agencies (website, marketing, email communications, for example) or have existing agencies, how will they work together? Full-service agencies have an obvious advantage if you work across media.

15 Negotiate – finally, don't forget that in a competitive, new-media climate, you can afford to be very demanding during negotiations.

Further information

www.revolution.haynet.com
www.webdesign.co.uk
www.ukwda.org (Web Design Association)

Ask a company if its website is accessible to those with vision, mobility or hearing disabilities and they'll probably tell you they haven't even thought about it. Ask them to make their site more accessible and they'll tell you that it would cost too much, for such a small minority.

This is why so many sites are impossible to use by the disabled, as they are not formatted for the specialist software or **browsers** they use. To do so would not only create a loyal user base but also is increasingly important as a greater percentage of the population grows older. But, under the Disability Discrimination Act, companies may now have a legal, not just moral obligation to make their site accessible. Lawsuits have already taken place in the US, e.g. that between the National Federation of the Blind and AOL, AOL having to settle out of court.

It is a misconception that making your site disabled-friendly is automatically expensive, especially if you build in the changes from the start.

The solution

Knowing your user and their software has never been more important than with accessibility. Software or browsers that increase text and image sizes are used by the visually impaired. Using absolute font sizes on web pages or italic text should therefore be avoided. Screen readers which translate pages to audio are also widely used. Pages that use **JavaScript** don't summarise images or graphics or forget to label buttons and render the screen reader useless. You can see how difficult your site is to use by downloading a free trial copy of IBM's Home Page Reader and trying it for yourself.

Testing your site with the disabled is essential. In May 2001, Tesco was the first supermarket to launch a separate site accessible to the visually impaired. It involved months of testing with visually impaired users and was given the first website award from the Royal National Institute for the Blind. Yet Tesco has realised greater rewards as a result – the simpler, reformatted site transferred more easily to other digital platforms and allowed Tesco to work on a service for Microsoft Pocket PCs.

There is a range of comprehensive guidelines to disabled accessibility online that every company should read. The most authoritative is the W3C Web

Accessibility Initiative. Making your website accessible is all about providing suitable alternatives and, if cost is an issue, retailers in particular need to remember — it's a lot less expensive to make a website accessible, than it is to refit every one of your offline stores.

Further information

www.ibm.com (search on 'home page reader')
www.tesco.com/access
www.w3.org/WAI
Web Accessibility for People with Disabilities (useful book by Paciello)
Mistake 12 – Lack of usability evaluation, see p. 24

76 Auction mismanagement

The mistake   Design   **Marketing**   Strategy

Despite European online consumer auctions being worth over €1 billion in 2001, the majority of business-to-consumer sites have not met the expectation that an auction is an instant success.

Initially, companies use auctions as a clearing mechanism for surplus stock. However, regular use of this approach implies there is something wrong with existing distribution channels and can create a late-buying market. Companies also have to be careful of damaging existing offline supply channels, which still produce the majority of revenue. There have also been high-profile auction casualties such as News International's FiredUp.com, launched in a blaze of publicity in December 1999 only to close sixteen months later.

There are questions over auctions' ability to maintain loyal customers. Research has shown that newcomers often only want to see what auction sites are like, but have no real interest in them. Overall, auctions can be an excellent distribution channel but many companies do not realise that setting up, monitoring and fulfilling auctions takes up considerable resources.

The solution

Not all products can be sold effectively by auction. It is no surprise that products such as electronics with fixed specifications and prices auction better than more complex high-value items. In travel this explains the early success of short-haul auctions from the likes of British Midland and Lufthansa and why long-haul airlines such as British Airways have been more cautious, testing auctions subtly via third parties like Lastminute.com. Certain types of auction (e.g. reverse, where prices are bid down) only work with high-volume transactions and products with relatively high margins.

You also need to decide whether to host auctions on your own site or follow many companies and become a merchant partner on high-volume third-party sites such as QXL.com. Small companies can run their own auctions by buying off-the-shelf software. Specialist software suppliers such as FairMarket service larger companies.

Fraud is a particular problem with auctions, accounting for up to two-thirds of reported Internet fraud. Auction sites need to promote credibility. Auction items must be honestly represented with a list of frequently asked questions and ideally the normal/retail price. In addition, if a minimum price is set at the start of the auction, it must offer real value.

Auctions will continue to play a significant role in e-commerce and are ideal for price-testing new products or markets. However, most companies do not yet see auctions as a main revenue stream and need to put resources into testing their true usefulness.

Further information

www.auctionwatch.com (has a useful auction news and information section)
www.fairmarket.com

77 Deep linking

The mistake

It would be rare to find a website without links but the universal practice of linking is changing given the predominance of commercial websites. 'Deep linking' occurs when a site links to a page in another site, which is not the home page but embedded further into the navigation.

Although links are the basis of the success of major portals such as Yahoo! certain types of link can cause problems. If site A links to site B, problems occur when:

- Site B's content is altered or removed or the computer code is changed when it is displayed after linking from site A
- Site A misleads users, by making it look like they own the content
- When site A uses **frames** to display site B's content. This makes B's web address hidden so users cannot see or remember it
- The link allows users to bypass pages on B's site which bypass income streams such as banner advertising or registration. Bypassing the home page is a problem as it usually commands the highest advertising revenues.

The solution

There is confusion over deep linking as there have been few legal cases globally to help set guidelines. A European legal precedent was set by UK recruitment-site stepstone.co.uk when it successfully stopped a rival German recruitment site linking to their jobs. StepStone successfully argued that the German site was using the link to substantiate claims about the number of jobs on its own site and the link bypassed advertising on StepStone's home page. The case used the European Directive on Legal Protection of Databases which prohibits the re-use of database content, which is what the link was effectively doing.

In France, the first such case was also between two recruitment firms (Keljob and Cadres Online) whereby Keljob linked to the other site's jobs but modified their web code and changed the page navigation. In both cases the issue involved infringement of copyright and intellectual property.

For a site linking to another there are several key points to consider:

- Before any link follow the rules of **netiquette** and ask permission, acknowledging linked content where necessary

- Avoid the use of frames. If they must be used confine to a small horizontal top frame to allow users to return to the original site. Alternatively, open up links in a new full browser window
- Make it clear when a user is leaving a site and linking to another
- Check a site's terms and conditions. Many are putting in clauses to cover deep linking and these should be carefully checked.

Overall consider:

- Level – how far into the other site does the link go?
- Motivation – why is a site linking. Is it to avoid having to create the content itself?
- Company – most of the legal cases so far have been brought against direct competitors.

Deep linking is an unclear and controversial topic. But, until it is clarified in law, sites need to be very careful if they want to avoid being the next test legal case.

Links

Mistake 35 – Copyright infringement, *see p. 70*
Mistake 61 – Frames, *see p. 122*

As in the offline world, people do not like completing online forms. Forms are required as part of the e-commerce process, when registering for premium content or gathering demographic information. However, forms create an interruption in the user experience and need to be carefully designed to encourage reluctant users to enter personal information. There are a number of common mistakes:

- Requiring registration too early in a site's navigation
- Asking for too much personal information before establishing trust
- Asking for the same data more than once
- Long continuous forms that look overwhelming
- Long drop-down menus to enter data
- Forcing users to answer questions that they think are irrelevant
- Negative and unclear error messages.

Sites relying on e-commerce and advertising revenue use forms to gather important personal data – so poor form design has a direct impact on revenue streams.

The solution

Set objectives
You must have a clear understanding of what you will do with the data you collect. Don't just copy what your competitors are doing; unused data adds useless questions to forms.

Benefit
Internet users are goal-orientated so be clear what the benefit will be to them of completing the form, and communicate this from the outset.

Push back registration
Unless your content is relatively unique don't put registration too early in your site's navigation. Users will not have enough information to understand the benefit of your site and will go elsewhere.

Break up pages

If you have a long form it is best to break it into pages or steps. Make it clear how many steps there are and how long it will take to complete them all.

Stagger data capture

To reduce the length of forms it is better to ask a minimum of questions at the outset to secure a registration and then ask further questions over time as users interact with your site. This will build up a broader picture of your users and ensure that if first registration was a long time ago, the data does not become dated.

Intuition

Users understand forms they have used elsewhere on the web so don't try and reinvent the process. If your form is intuitive to use and the questions follow a logical order you will not need much explanatory text – which many users never read properly anyway.

Usernames and passwords

Cause a lot of confusion unless you are clear what characters can be used and whether capital letters are recognised. A 'password reminder' feature is essential.

Legal

Ensure you include buttons to opt in or out of company or partner communications, in line with the Data Protection Act. It is also good practice to include a link to your privacy policy.

Error messages

Are very important and need to be written clearly by copywriters, not by the web designers who built the form.

Recognise

One of users' greatest annoyances is being asked the same question twice so design systems (e.g. using **cookies**) that can recognise users when they return to your site.

Further information

www.formsthatwork.com (excellent resource on form usability)
Mistake 93 – Confusing error messages, *see p. 186*
Mistake 13 – Ignoring the Data Protection Act, *see p. 26*

79 Banner exchanges

The mistake

Banner exchanges are communities of website owners that agree to swap banners on a contra basis in order to promote each other's sites. They are popular with smaller sites with no online marketing budget or limited staff as the idea is free, simple, automatic and is expected to drive traffic.

But the practicalities of banner exchanges make them ineffective. Exchange networks manage the community of sites but charge a commission. To get one banner displayed on another community site, you must generally display two banners, often in prominent page positions such as top of page. This extra banner is the network's commission, which it sells to paid-for advertisers. Another problem is that you have limited control over the type and quality of adverts appearing on your site. Conversely, when your banner is shown on another site, it is unlikely to be well targeted and may even be globally served. Your banner may only show once on one of thousands of sites, reducing the effect of repeat viewings and branding.

The 2:1 ratio also means that smaller sites must have a reasonable volume of traffic in the first place, which queries the goal of using exchanges to build traffic. If targeting is limited and the alternative of branding cannot be guaranteed, their use is therefore questionable.

The solution

If you wish to test banner exchanges then it is wise to check out the many networks on offer. All have different terms and some offer better ratios (e.g. 4:3 from LinkBuddies) or exchanges based on click through rather than number of banners served.

A preferred option is to set up your own barter deal with another site. Given the slow down in the advertising industry during 2001, sites have a lot more unsold inventory so are willing to try contra advertising. Your own barter allows you to approach like-minded sites and work on a fairer ratio. Normally barters are calculated based on the advertising **ratecard** and will only be on a 1:1 ratio if the ratecard value of the buy is the same on both sides. Bartering with a few rather than thousands of sites as with exchanges, will also increase the frequency that the same audience sees your banner. It is always worth monitoring barters in case the partner site gives a paid for advertiser priority or fails to report back the results of the campaign.

With average banner **click through rates** below 0.5 per cent even for paid-for targeted campaigns, banner exchanges with their 2:1 ratios produce even worse results. Banner exchanges rely on the idea that great results can be achieved online for free, a premise that with the likes of search-engine listings and **viral marketing** continues to be widespread. But as the Internet becomes a crowded place, the poor performance of banner exchanges is just another example that, like offline, effective advertising requires investment.

Further information

www.yahoo.com (search on 'banner exchanges' for a comprehensive list)
www.bcentral.com/services/bn (Microsoft's bCentral exchange network)
www.linkbuddies.com

80 3D shopping

The mistake

Compared to offline stores, one of the main problems with online shopping is that it is two dimensional. For certain products, such as CDs for example, this is not a problem. But for items like cars, furniture and clothing, 2D takes away the ability to touch and try out a product before purchase.

However, 3D shopping processes have been an attempt to bridge this gap. Customers can try on clothing, zoom in on product pictures or take 360° photographic tours. Or, 3D can be used as a navigational tool to move around a site.

But the process has not lived up to the hype it created several years ago. Three key problems remain:

- Internet bandwidth restrictions make the process slow and low quality
- The process can take up a lot of PC memory making users' PCs more likely to crash
- Most users need non-standard **plug-ins** to view.

The most celebrated case of the failure of the 3D-shopping process was the original sportswear retailer Boo.com in 2000. Questions asked then are still relevant – is 3D shopping just a gimmick, that does more for PR than it does for actual sales?

The solution

The offline–online gap in 3D retailing is still not bridged, given the poor quality and small size of 3D products. Several thumbnail-sized product pictures from different angles that can be enlarged, will give the same all-round view without the cost and need for user plug-ins. It is also questionable whether many products actually benefit from 3D. Customers know what a shirt looks like and still can't touch it with a 3D view.

Price also affects the attractiveness of 3D shopping. Customers have less time to research low-value products, so then 3D becomes a distraction, but they have more patience for high-value products such as cars. Even in this case, 3D graphics will facilitate the sale but won't guarantee it if price is a determining factor.

Even if a 3D-shop provides an entertaining experience to the first-time visitor, repeat customers quickly tire of the effect as they focus more on their

160

buying goals. Many sites therefore limit 3D to pan or zoom effects on product photographs which do not require user plug-ins. Marksandspencer.com, for example, shows lifestyle shots of its clothes on models. Users can then click to get a close up view of the individual garment.

3D shopping is becoming more manageable with the introduction of **broadband** Internet connections, cheaper and better graphics compression software and faster PCs, such as those with the Intel Pentium 4 chip with improved handling of 3D graphics and video **streaming**. However, 3D shopping shouldn't be implemented just because it can be. When retailer Fashionmall revived the collapsed Boo.com, it reportedly purchased everything except the 3D software which quickened its original demise. Until the majority of user systems can cope with 3D shopping, the significant investment is best spent on more detailed, higher quality product descriptions, returns policies and improved customer service.

Further information

Mistake 58 – Animation over information, see p. 116
Mistake 55 – Poor product information, see p. 110

81 Long scrolling pages

Having to scroll web pages is inevitable given that, unlike designing a printed page, there is no control over a user's screen resolution or the size of the **browser** window they are using. However, long scrolling pages are not recommended for a number of reasons:

- Users scan web pages – long pages make this difficult
- Users are less likely to see content further down the page, in deciding on the relevance of the page and the site
- Scrolling down can lose navigation and reference points higher up the page, so it is harder to make comparative judgements. This is unless you use **frames** but these aren't always recommended
- Long pages increase page file size, so they take longer to download.

Many sites try to stick to the '3-click rule', whereby all content is no more than three clicks away from any page. For large sites, this encourages cramming too much content onto individual pages. Companies with small budgets are also tempted to make pages too long, if they have a lot of content and their contract to build the site is based on a limited number of pages.

Users are beginning to accept scrolling, but this is more a result of experience than preference.

The solution

Screen resolution
Designing a site for too high a screen resolution will make pages too long or require horizontal scrolling if users view them with low-resolution monitors. The majority of sites are designed for 600×800 resolution which accounts for just over half of all monitor settings.

Break up screens
The simple solution to long pages is to break them up, as long as it is clear how all the individual sections link together. Some of the most successful registration forms and e-commerce shopping carts use this approach, by breaking up user interaction into separate manageable tasks.

Experience or retrieval

You can determine the length of pages by thinking of them as either aids to experience or retrieval. Experience pages can be highly branded but must be short with clear signposts, signals and summarised content, such as your home page. Retrieval pages are where the detailed content of your site sits, are further down the navigational structure and can therefore afford to be longer. Long documents or brochures on retrieval pages may be best made available as downloadable **PDF** or Word files.

Top of page

If your pages require scrolling then keep the most important content near the top. Visual clues can then be used to encourage users to scroll downwards.

A general rule is to limit scrolling to a maximum of two–three pages. New devices are also available to help users cope better with scrolling – such as the 'intelligent mouse' with a scroll wheel fitted or flat screen monitors that can view web pages in portrait as well as landscape mode. Content is also increasingly re-purposed to run across other platforms, such as **WAP** and handheld devices, where small screen size dictates that pages must be short.

Determining page length is subjective and dependent on a number of factors – overall it's a matter of balance.

82 Credit-card chargebacks

Research shows that anywhere between 25 and 50 per cent of consumers say Internet credit-card fraud is a worry. Their fear has been heightened by high-profile cases of unauthorised access to customer credit-card details by companies like Powergen and Barclays Bank. However, the reality is that in most cases it is the merchant company, not the consumer that picks up the cost.

> A survey during 2000 showed that 20 per cent of UK companies suffer chargebacks in excess of 1 per cent of sales and 85 per cent don't have automated fraud protection systems.
>
> *Source*: Experian

E-commerce companies don't have procedures in place to detect online fraud and often use inaccurate manual processes. It can take over a month before they realise a transaction is fraudulent, and then must refund the loss as well as an administration fee, known as a 'chargeback'.

However, there are a number of simple measures that can be taken to reduce fraud. If companies ignore them and fraud occurs regularly, then they are at serious risk of losing their merchant account from their bank.

The solution

Validate customers
An online purchase is similar to a telephone 'card not present' purchase. You need to verify the card-holder's address. Companies such as Experian or Retail Decisions offer real-time verification services. Another simple rule is only to deliver to the card-holder's address, or ask for a fax of the card and signature if another address is requested.

Look out for clues
There are obvious clues to fraudulent purchases. Purchases from countries such as Eastern Europe and the Far East are statistically more likely to be fraudulent. You should also be wary of unusually large orders. Some US companies also refuse to process cards from 'free' or portal email accounts, as fraudsters can easily use them.

Digital certificates

Secure certificate programmes such as those from Verisign can be purchased, which not only assist you in ensuring your **server** is secure, but also are becoming recognised by consumers as a sign of security, which helps to create trust.

Secure portals

There are an increasing number of secure shopping portals such as Securicor's safedoor.co.uk which process customer credit-card details securely on retailers' behalf and then forward them the sale less a commission. Although populated mainly by large retailers they are likely to become increasingly popular. They effectively manage e-wallets on behalf of customers, similar to Microsoft's Passport system, which you can add easily to your site.

Non-digital processes

Another solution is combining online with offline services. Customers may prefer to give order and basic personal details online, and then pay for the transaction over the phone or in-store. This gives the added benefit of human customer service to ensure the sale completes.

As the major banks and governments work towards better standards, merchants will have a better choice of solutions. Nonetheless, you will always have to accept some degree of risk, but there's a lot you can do to minimise it.

Further information

www.verisign.com
www.experian.com
www.retaildecisions.com
www.microsoft.com/uk/passport
Mistake 14 – No online-payment system, *see p. 28*

83 No competitive-intelligence strategy

The Internet has changed the speed and the gathering of competitive intelligence. But, with limited time and an overwhelming number of online information sources, keeping to a formalised competitor-monitoring process is difficult.

> Only 11 per cent of UK companies conduct external Internet e-business intelligence.
>
> *Source:* Cyveillance International, Sept 2000

Intelligence can give you a head start on your competitors. For example, in July 2000, Coca-Cola launched their successful cokeauction.com site, where customers could bid with Coke ring-pulls in cashless auctions. Their competitors could have had warning of this, if they had been notified that Coke first registered the **domain** name five months earlier.

There is a wealth of competitor-information online, you just need to know where to look.

The solution

Online press clippings
You should keep an eye on online newspapers, **newsgroups**, trade websites and search engines for your competitors. Companies such as CyberAlert can do this for you or a free option is to sign up to several news tracker services, which search on keywords. Excite's NewsTracker service is a good example.

Patents and trademarks
Considerable information is available online for free. The Patent Office's European espacenet database allows you to search patents by company name; whilst the UK Patent Office website allows you to search their trade-mark records.

Stock prices
Can be monitored by a huge number of sites and reported back to you automatically. FTMarketWatch.com is a good example.

Website updates
You can download a range of free or inexpensive software from directories such as shareware.com, that will track any page on the Internet (including your competitors) and alert you when anything changes. Useful for monitoring product or price changes.

Usability testing
Don't confine user testing to your own site. If your competitor launches a new online tool (e.g. shopping cart) you can ask how users would improve it before building your own.

Company reports
Can be viewed at a range of sites, such as the popular Hoovers.com

Domain monitoring
You can register with companies such as NetNames.com who offer a domain/web-address monitoring service based on keywords. You can enter your competitors' names and brands to see when they register new addresses.

Recruitment
It is also worth registering your competitors' names as keywords on recruitment sites' email alerts. Another chance to keep ahead of new roles or departments.

Specialists
There are a number of companies that specialise in gathering this information for you, such as Cyveillance. However, their services can be relatively expensive.

Further information

www.cyberalert.com
nt.excite.com
www.espacenet.com
www.patent.gov.uk
www.cyveillance.co.uk (includes useful 'white paper' reports)
Mistake 26 – Poor quality PR, see p. 52
Mistake 12 – Lack of usability evaluation, see p. 24

84 Creative accounting

For many new dot com companies, their valuations and success have been built on the promise of future sales and returns rather than real assets or profits. Reporting rising revenues has a significant impact on stock prices, PR, customer confidence and the ability to gain further funding. It may be no surprise, then, to hear accusations of 'creative' accounting levied at dot com companies.

This has been especially true in the US. Back in May 2000, AOL were forced to pay a $3.5 million penalty by the SEC (Securities & Exchange Commission) for inaccurate financial reporting which helped to show profits, rather than losses for six quarters. The problem is that, on both sides of the Atlantic, the Internet has created similar needs for new accounting methods, given the many grey areas – grey areas that too many executives are tempted to exploit.

The solution

There are a number of areas that dot coms have exploited to boost their revenues and financial performance:

Barter transactions

In particular advertising barter, such as banners. This occurs when a company signs a contra deal with another advertiser and reports the value of the contra as actual revenue. Although traditional companies have always used barter, it has only been a small percentage of their overall revenue, not up to half, as has been the case for some dot coms.

Discount coupons

Especially digital versions; these are a popular way to drive sales. However, a number of high-profile brands report the full price of a discounted sale and quote the coupon value as a 'marketing expense'. Fulfilment costs are another expenditure that have been classified as 'marketing expenses' and not costs of sale. The overall result is higher reported revenues.

Intermediaries

For example, online travel agents, who have been known to quote the value of their bookings as gross revenue (including supplier costs) and not report the much smaller commission they make. Their argument is that as they take the financial responsibility for the gross amount, that is what they should report.

Website costs

Another technique is to capitalise website planning and maintenance assets rather than charging them to the profit and loss account. The question is, are they really an asset?

The overall aim is to boost revenue. This can be done prematurely, such as when auction houses charge for listings and a commission on sales, then count the revenue immediately rather than when the goods have actually been delivered. The UK's ASB (Accounting Standards Board) has issued directives, stating that barter transactions are only permitted when there is evidence that 'if the advertising had not been exchanged, it would have been sold for cash in a similar transaction'. It has also issued guidelines as to how to capitalise website costs.

At the end of the day, these grey areas are a judgement call by management and auditors. Yet they need to remember that such creative accounting may result in having to restate earning or, even worse, a future down valuation in the company.

Further information

www.asb.org.uk
www.sec.gov

Since the 1990s, new media start-ups have helped to create different work and life-style expectations amongst employees. Companies, especially those with established organisational structures, have not been able to adapt as quickly and have suffered an exodus of staff to dot com companies with better working conditions and higher salaries.

Despite high-profile redundancies during the market downturn since 2000, the speed at which employees are changing jobs is increasing. Companies are making the mistake of being slow to adapt to these changes, believing salary to be the only motivator and not accepting that even medium-term loyalty is increasingly rare.

As many executives are now leaving new media to return to more stable industries, they bring back with them new working principles. Companies must react to these if they are to keep staff longer than until the next upturn in the industry.

The solution

Hiring
Gartner Group estimate that by 2003, 60 per cent of enterprises will revamp their hiring processes to remedy IT skills shortages. Currently, interview processes look at the long-term prospects of interviewees, which is no longer relevant. The importance is not what an interviewee has done or for how long, but how they did it. New recruits must be able to get up to speed – there is no time for long 'probationary' periods. They must be multi-skilled – technical and commercial departments can no longer work in isolation.

Environment
Beyond the casual dress and 'pool table' in every office, new media has created more flexible and motivating cultures. Online-bank Egg.com won a digital office award in 2001 for this approach. It need not be costly but it does require a change of attitude.

Organisational structure
Successful new-media companies bring their technical and creative teams together. Open-plan offices and a less obvious hierarchy are the norm. Larger

enterprises can think that a more flexible e-business structure will clash with the culture of other departments. Yet companies using this approach (such as British Airways' eBA department) report few problems, with lower staff turnover and improved performance.

Capital incentives
Stock options no longer have the same appeal given market downturns, but regular incentive schemes for all staff help increase motivation. More Internet-only companies are offering pensions, which is also an indication that they are committing to new media for the long term.

New expectations
Companies must understand that new media staff are far more likely to take career risks and look for skills development and experience as opposed to earnings alone. The willingness to move easily, means that training and performance reviews need to occur more regularly, if you want to keep staff longer.

Overall, you might think the cost of making these changes prohibitive. But high staff turnover is now a fact of life in new media – ignore this fact and the cost of recruitment could be a lot higher.

Further information

www.onrec.com (Internet recruitment news)
www.interviewer-magazine.co.uk (weekly recruitment news)

86 Wireless spam

The mistake

Tremendous growth in wireless marketing is expected over the next five years with **WAP**, handheld and, in particular, **SMS** messaging. This is unsurprising, given that a fifth of European mobile users already send up to ten SMS text messages per day. However, the industry is very much in its infancy and, although there has been little **spamming** so far, it is a real concern.

Marketers need to avoid using web tactics. Mobile messages do not have email subject lines so are always read and are much more personal. You get them wrong at the expense of your brand reputation. Test surveys have produced high response rates of over 60 per cent but these have been with recognised companies such as McDonalds and Thomas Cook. When lesser-known brands use mobile messaging, the inevitable bulk messaging occurs and the novelty wears thin. Users will then start to switch off.

i-mode, the advanced Japanese mobile network, had to launch a campaign in summer 2001 to help combat huge growth in wireless spam. Marketers need to learn from such experiences as similar outbreaks are possible in Europe.

The solution

Gaining permission to message is not a new concept but is vital for this media. Permission is required for what, when and how messages are received. Opt-out mechanisms are more complicated but necessary, although in 2001 there was confusion as to their enforceability under the Data Protection Act. Message frequency and timing needs managing; marketers should aim for high-value and low-volume campaigns.

Effective low-volume campaigns mean improved targeting. The effect of immediate incentives and gratification with mobile messaging means that if you don't have the technology to target you must use a more subtle approach. There has been experimentation with messaging in return for payments, especially call discounts. No one is sure if this will work, but bear in mind the failure of similar web-based ventures. Customers want something for free but don't want to be annoyed. This will be all the more relevant with the introduction of 3G/more advanced mobile phones, which will be able to stream constant rich-media or video messages.

The Wireless Advertising Association has drawn up guidelines for wireless marketing to improve credibility, including maximum characters for different types of text message. They are also looking to agree with mobile operators a number of response metrics so you can measure the effectiveness of your campaigns.

At present, you need to approach your advertising agency, or specialist agencies such as Flytext.co.uk, to implement wireless campaigns, or it may be wise to wait for the big brands to test the process before getting involved. One thing is for sure – Internet advertising initially produced a pattern of novelty, high-response rates, spam and then calls for better targeting. So there are no excuses for repeating these mistakes in the wireless domain.

Further information

www.wirelessmarketing.org.uk (Wireless Marketing Association)
www.waaglobal.org (Wireless Advertising Association)
Mistake 13 – Ignoring the Data Protection Act, see p. 26
Mistake 10 – Spam, see p. 20

87 Time-insensitive marketing

The Internet offers 24-hour access regardless of time zone and has quickened the development of the time-precious consumer. Online customers' expectations have advanced rapidly and they now require faster Internet access, fast-loading web pages, immediate customer service and quicker delivery. Despite this, few online marketers use time to make their campaigns more effective.

Time-sensitive marketing is all about better targeting. A major reason that it is not widely practised is that companies do not have sophisticated enough online-profiling techniques to monitor user behaviour.

TV and radio media have long determined prices based on the time of day (e.g. peak viewing times) and there is scope for the success of this approach to be translated to the Internet.

The solution

You don't have to have expensive database software to experiment with simple online time marketing. Every site-statistics package such as WebTrends breaks down traffic by time of day, most sites experiencing the usual peaks around lunchtime and early evening. Despite the need for dynamic content and home pages to improve site 'stickiness', few sites alter their content by time of day or day of the week. Heinz have tried this approach with lovelunch.com, a site aimed at workers surfing during lunchtimes; the site can only be accessed between 11am and 3pm.

Targeting online advertising should also use time of day, and creatives can be altered to appeal to different users if the media owner can provide sufficient user profiles. Campaigns can also be optimised in real time to serve only at times of the day when click through is highest.

Email communications can also benefit. A regular e-newsletter can be sent out at different times of the day and week to monitor response. It will depend on content – entertainment-based messages perform better for example, if sent on Friday afternoon rather than Monday morning. If your userbase is global then international time zones need to be considered.

Spotting user trends based on time allows retailers to predict user behaviour and hence serve more relevant content. The Engage company, for example, offers 'Audience Insight Reports' which monitor the profiles of users who visit your site and also the other sites they visit on the Internet. This can show trends over time, which can be used to anticipate subsequent purchases. However, get this functionality wrong and the message becomes more irritating than helpful.

The move towards personalisation and the success of customised content such as myBBC or myYahoo! take time marketing to an individual level. However, understanding how time affects response can be tested and achieved simply, even without such levels of sophistication. Time certainly is money when it comes to the effectiveness of online marketing.

Further information

www.lovelunch.com
www.engage.com
Mistake 89 – Designing for users rather than buyers, see p. 178

When a site focuses on improving its search-engine rankings there is no guarantee of success. There is the perception that effective search engineering can be achieved with low-cost or simple procedures. In reality, effective ranking costs, whether that is in terms of internal resource or if an external company manages the process.

> Sites found via search engines make up 55 per cent of online purchases compared with 9 per cent found via banner adverts.
>
> *Source*: NPD Group, February 2001

Effective ranking can now be purchased as advertising. Not only does this offer an easy way to target consumers, but many are offered on pay-per-performance models, so you only pay when someone clicks on your advert. Although there has been debate over 'pure' search engines against those 'tainted' by advertising, users rarely see the difference and it could be that all search engines in the future will offer this approach in one way or another.

The solution

There are two main types of search-engine advertising to consider:

Keyword advertising
Most search engines will serve banners or other advertising based on the keywords users enter when searching. Most of the major search engines offer this service but the price can be up to three times that of standard run-of-site banners. Google offers a similar 'AdWord' service which serves keyword-text adverts to the right of the results page. If more users click on your advert then it gets a higher positioning on the page. The whole process can be managed online and purchased using a credit card.

Keyword placement
In this case you pay an amount per click for your ranking in the main results page of a search. The more you pay, the higher you rank and, since you pay only when someone clicks on your site, it also gives you some free branding for all

the occasions that they don't. Overture.com (formerly GoTo.com) and espotting.com are two sites that offer this service.

The real benefit of keywords is that they can offer very specific targeting. Look at your own website statistics to see what keywords brought users to your site from search-engine referrals, or consider buying commonly mis-spelt words. You will also achieve better response if you tailor each advert creative to each set of keywords. Some will even allow you to target by both country and language.

Some search engines also have conditions to protect their users. Google will not link to sites that disable the 'Back' **browser** button (often caused by **Flash** software) or that produce multiple pop-up windows. Also ensure the search engine has procedures to spot invalid clicking, such as competitors repeatedly selecting your advert, knowing that you pay for every click.

Paying for search-engine placements can be a cost-effective way to target your users and is ideal if you have a niche website with a limited advertising budget.

Further information

www.adwords.google.com
www.payperclicksearchengines.com (review of all major search engines)
Mistake 11 – Lack of a search-engine strategy, see p. 22

89 Designing for users rather than buyers

When a website adds e-commerce functionality, it designs for users or customers who want to purchase online. If customers are segmented, it is usually in terms of how much they spend rather than their buying situation.

This explains the poor shopper-to-buyer conversion rates. Different users have different buying goals and, aside from general demographic information, sites need to be tailored to help buyers achieve them.

The solution

The time a user has been online directly affects their willingness to buy. New users lack confidence and are the most concerned about security and privacy issues. Forcing registration on these users is likely to be unsuccessful and they need clear explanation of the benefits of buying online. Most online users will take two years before they make their first purchase and these will be for small defined products. This has implications for how an online bookseller, for example, should present itself compared to a financial-service provider.

The stage at which a user is in the buying process is also important:

Window shopper

Window shoppers are browsers with no clear idea of what they want. This group responds well to welcome tours, site maps, best-seller lists and promotions, such as the 'what's hot' section of department store debenhams.com. With time to surf they are more tolerant of entertainment or visual distractions if they help them learn more about products or stimulate ideas.

Information seeker

The next stage of the process is when a buyer decides on the product category but needs more information. Here detailed product information and comparisons are welcome, as are independent or consumer reviews. The buyer is more receptive to cross-selling or packaged solutions that offer value and to marketing of non-product benefits such as delivery speed or after-sales service guarantees.

Ready to buy

According to the Online Culture Survey 2001 (from the UK's Henley Centre and Royal Mail), it is estimated that four out of five people have a specific interest in mind before they go online. Those that know what they want to buy need direct access to the e-commerce process, along with the latest promotions, to ensure they are getting the best deal before they commit to a purchase. As well as 'what's hot', debenhams.com also offers an 'express purchase' function off the home page. This is not the place for large pages with slow download times nor links or distractions to other pages or websites. Security and privacy guarantees are important, as is explaining the full shopping process from the outset.

As well as the stage in the buying process, the Online Culture Survey also showed that location such as home or office affects mood and therefore willingness to buy. Time is also an issue. Office workers will, for example, be more willing to window shop at lunchtimes or after work than in the morning.

Smart websites are already realising that to improve buyer-conversion rates, they not only need to target users, they also need to target the users' state of mind.

Further information

Mistake 87 – Time-insensitive marketing, see p. 174

90 Lack of coupon marketing

Discount coupons traditionally have never been seen as cutting-edge promotional tools and many companies are still of the mindset that they only appeal to fast-moving consumer goods or to an older demographic. However, the Internet has revolutionised the ease and speed at which coupons can be distributed and redeemed and are becoming a vital link between online and offline stores.

> E-coupon usage is growing in the US. A study of Internet users showed 20 per cent have already downloaded e-coupons. Consumers are also twice as likely to download coupons from the Internet and then redeem them offline, rather than online.
>
> *Source*: Cyber Dialogue, May 2001

Despite concerns regarding security and over-redemption, coupons can be a cost-effective way to prospect for new customers, build databases, generate sales and meet customer expectations that online products should be less expensive than offline.

The solution

Online to offline coupons
Customers print out the coupon from a website themselves. Either staff can accept the printed coupon or it can have a bar code printed on it, which can be scanned by the store till. However, barcodes are dependent on the quality of the customer's printer. Given that over 50 per cent of customers are estimated to research online but purchase offline, they also provide a vital link between the two channels.

Offline to online coupons
As well as building website awareness, traffic and data capture, offline to online coupons can be profitable if the discount is less than the cost per transaction saving of selling online.

Online to online coupons

They require the most technical investment in order to ensure security, although this can be outsourced to companies such as e-centives or online-incentives. However, the investment will soon pay for itself, saving the cost of traditional coupon printing and distribution.

Wireless coupons

An increasing number of sites are testing **WAP** or **SMS** text-based coupons, which appeal to a younger audience. Bacardi have used them to send two-for-one drinks' offers – recipients then showed their phone screen to bar staff to redeem.

Portals

There are a number of coupon portals which offer mainly online to offline coupons. In the US, Coolsavings.com is the largest with over 14 million registered members. In the UK, couponsnow.co.uk and freecoupons.co.uk offer coupons from companies such as Burger King, Radisson Edwardian Hotels and the RAC.

If you don't have the technology securely and uniquely to stamp each coupon then you have little control over consumers passing them on and must factor in higher redemption rates. Over reliance on coupons isn't wise as price-only promotions are unlikely to build long-term loyalty. However, even if you are not prepared to invest in integrating coupon redemption into your database, even simple printable coupons should be considered as part of your overall marketing strategy.

Further information

www.e-centives.com
www.online-incentives.co.uk

91 Browser incompatibility

The mistake | Design Marketing Strategy

A website can be viewed on an increasing number of devices. Although Internet Explorer dominates in the PC market, there are many different versions as well as numerous handheld computer, web TV and net-enabled games console devices. A well-designed site can quickly fall down if not fully tested on all these platforms.

Sites regularly receive bugs and technical errors from users due to lack of testing. Testing costs time and money, an area where external agencies can not only easily cut costs but also keep ongoing as new versions of devices are released. Designers might blame manufacturers for developing non-standard devices but, if an error occurs, it reflects badly on site owners. For users, it is a lot easier to use another website than another device.

The solution

Internet Explorer has beaten Netscape in the **browser** wars with an estimated share of over 85 per cent. A small percentage is taken up by lesser-known browsers such as Mosaic or Mozilla for Mac computers. The latest versions all have new features, and sites should be wary of using features specific to one browser only. Internet Explorer 6 for example has clearer **cookie** notification, which will affect how sites monitor user behaviour. Designers must test sites on all browser versions and online tools (such as from Net Mechanic or Any Browser) can quickly highlight errors and also have features to test sites for different monitor screen resolutions.

Web TV has long been available in the US and was recently introduced in the UK with devices such as the Bush Internet TV. Any website can be viewed through these devices. The difference is the distance from which users sit from a TV screen compared with a monitor. Normal websites cannot be viewed effectively on TV resolution screens and need to be re-purposed with larger fonts and graphics, reduced scrolling and contrasting colours. Alternatively, handheld devices require short pages with simple navigation. Whereas handheld computers used to involve specially created content such as an AvantGo channel, devices such as the Compaq iPAQ can view normal web pages. But, unless sites are re-purposed, they will be incompatible for its smaller screen size. Emulators such as the Palm Operating System Emulator and WebTV Viewer are a quick way to test compatibility on these devices.

Site statistics will indicate the browsers and devices that users currently have to determine the extent of testing and, if this is a web agency's responsibility, it would be wise to agree levels of compatibility from the start. For non-PC devices such as handheld computers, re-purposing or creating different versions of a site is currently the best way to ensure compatibility – although this can be costly. It is impossible to create 100 per cent compatibility but with users increasingly demanding multi-channel content, you need to balance producing an error-free website for the majority of your users, against the alternative of having to create a bland site, designed for lower-version devices.

Further information

www.netmechanic.com
www.anybrowser.com
www.statmarket.com (latest statistics on browser usage)
www.bushinternet.com
www.palmos.com/dev/tech/tools/emulator
developer.msntv.com

As Internet access becomes more mainstream, the demographic of users has moved away from the young, educated early adopters of the mid to late nineties. It is estimated that over 5 million older people (or the 'grey' market) are online and they represent the fastest growing Internet demographic.

Despite the growth in 'silver surfers', too many sites are youth-orientated. This is not surprising given that the majority of web designers, agency and new media staff are under 40. If sites do appreciate older users, they are usually badly targeted, as one homogenous 'over 50s' group. There are a number of portals that target the grey market such as www.fifthmoon.com and vavo.com, but the challenge to more general sites with a wider customer age range is to learn how to avoid alienating older users and tap into their vast e-commerce potential.

The solution

Studies show that the reason silver surfers go online in the first place is communication. Email is used by nine out of ten, often for keeping in touch with children and relatives, whilst other drivers are shopping, holidays, competitions, health, financial advice and, in particular, education and learning. The key difference with silver surfers is that not only do they have longer to spend online (an average of over nine hours a week according to Age Concern) but also higher disposable incomes and a greater propensity to purchase.

A marketer would never target the whole of the 'under 30' demographic and neither should everyone 'over 50' be grouped. Basing campaigns by splitting age range into decades (such as 50s, 60s) will improve response. In terms of site design, silver surfers are more conservative. They prefer clutter-free layouts and simple intuitive navigation. The busy, constantly updating and animated content of sites aimed at younger demographics do more to distract. Silver surfers are also more concerned about the privacy and security issues of the Internet. So addressing important design, navigation and confidence issues not only benefits all customers but particularly those with relatively more to spend.

It is true that the take up of new and emerging technologies such as interactive TV, wireless communication and messaging is by younger people, but on fixed-line Internet, silver surfers still represent a mostly untapped market, although in the past two years, some large corporations have woken up to their spending power. But, with over half of the population expected to be over 50 within the next 20 years, silver surfers won't be a demographic that can be ignored for too much longer.

Further information

www.ageconcern.co.uk
www.helptheaged.org.uk
   (Both sites have useful information and statistics.)

93 Confusing error messages

The mistake   Design   Marketing   Strategy

Error messages are common on websites, occurring when users make a mistake while entering or searching for data. They are most common with registration forms, login screens or during the shopping cart or sales process.

Problems occur because messages are written by technical designers rather than by copywriters. They are often also final, in the sense that users either understand and respond to the error or cannot proceed.

Executives might see error messages as trivial, but they are an unwelcome interruption in the user experience. Revenues are now so dependent on registration and e-commerce forms that a confusing message can make the difference between staying with a site or abandoning it and any potential sale.

The solution

Errors should be minimised by aiming to make navigation and data entry as simple and intuitive as possible. Form layout should follow a logical sequence and potentially confusing questions should have concise explanations or examples next to them. This is vital for password registration, where users need to understand whether passwords are valid in capital letters, lower case or both. Errors can also be minimised by forcing users to select options, such as drop-down boxes to choose an order delivery date, rather than typing freely.

Consideration needs to be given as to how error messages are displayed. Browser-alert boxes, which **pop-up** with the error message are an option, although can only show one error at a time. A preferable solution is to redisplay a submitted form with the incorrect areas highlighted and, importantly, a call to action – i.e. an explanation of what to do rather than just what is wrong. When redisplaying forms be sure to keep any data that was correctly entered to prevent the user having to type it all in again. The actual text of the error message also needs to be written concisely and politely by a copywriter.

Error messages should, where possible, provide an alternative solution in order to proceed. A good example is 'wrong password' error messages, which generally now include a 'password reminder' function, which resends the user's password to their registered email address. These could also include a frequent-error list, an email contact address or a link to a call centre so a transaction can be completed on the user's behalf.

Customers see error messages as a form of customer service, by helping them when things go wrong. They certainly wouldn't appreciate incomplete or confusing assistance from staff in an offline store but this is effectively what a poorly designed error message achieves online. It is inevitable that users will make errors online – sites need to ensure that error messages help them achieve their goals rather than stopping them abruptly in their tracks.

Further information

Mistake 17 – Broken links, see p. 34
Mistake 78 – Complex registration forms, see p. 156

Over-use of competitions

The Internet has revitalised competitions as a promotional tool by making them quick and easy to enter. Subsequently, companies are seeing them as the answer to all their traffic problems, assuming that running regular competitions creates loyalty. It is easy to run a competition badly, as there are many pitfalls:

- Attracting users who are more interested in competitions than your site or brand
- Regularly attracting existing users rather than acquiring new users
- Making competitions too complicated or requiring complex registration
- Unclear terms and conditions and lack of obvious privacy policies
- Non-communication of the results to entrants
- Slow fulfilment for large-scale competitions/promotions
- Adding a viral element to a competition and assuming it will promote itself

Avoiding pitfalls is important. In Summer 2000, Virgin Wines received criticism of a viral competition to win a holiday, as entry was conditional on nominating three friends to travel with you – some considered this technique as bad **netiquette**.

The solution

Objectives
The reason behind your competition will determine both its structure and promotion. There are several possible objectives:

Branding – a successful competition in this case must develop a relationship with your users. Entertainment and interactive options, which fit your brand, are ideal. Animated games are a popular choice.

Traffic – if you want to build traffic then your competition must be well-promoted and easy to enter.

Email/Registration – Entry by email address is a quick way to increase subscriptions to regular newsletters but, if you want more demographic information, your prize must reflect the value the user places on giving out more personal information.

Prize

Because there are so many competitions online, your prize must suit your target audience. If your site has sufficient traffic, many companies are willing to provide prizes in return for sponsorship. PR agencies or corporate incentive specialists can offer this service.

Rules

Terms and conditions are legally required and ideally should be checked by your legal team, especially if there will be US or global entrants. Terms must be 'downloadable' according to the Advertising Standards Authority so ensure this applies if running competitions on mobile or handheld devices. It is also good practice to add a privacy policy next to any data entry form.

Three other important considerations:

Communication – too often sites forget to show winners of competitions or email losers with some other form of discount or reward which could generate sales.

Fulfilment for one-off large-scale competitions needs careful planning and may be best outsourced to mailing houses.

Closed user groups, such as registered users or specific countries, should be carefully targeted to ensure you don't alienate other users who are not eligible.

Competitions are effective but don't rely on them too heavily. If they're the only way you can drive traffic or collect data, it indicates a low value for the rest of your site's content.

Further information

www.asa.org.uk (useful 'Sales Promotion Code' which covers competitions)
www.loquax.com (check out competitors' competitions on this UK portal)

95 Printer-unfriendly pages

Predictions of the paperless office as a result of e-filing have yet to materialise as users still like physically to print out documents and web pages. Traditional print and web media are very different. Layout, fonts and colours which may look great on screen, usually translate poorly offline. Printing and online brochureware can also provide a vital link between those users that use the Internet to research but then go offline to make a purchase. As a result, websites should look at how they can complement print media rather than trying to replace it.

The solution

Print button

Is a very simple function which re-purposes a web page into a printer-friendly version. However, there are still many sites that do not have this feature. Printer-friendly pages can also be a useful area for incremental sponsorship or advertising. Internet Explorer 5.5 and later versions also have a print preview button so users can check if a webpage is suitable for printing.

Other export options

The three other forms of saving page content are via email (e.g. 'send this page to a friend'), fax (although this is less common given the cost of calls) and, more recently, handheld computers. The latter is important as handheld devices allow greater portability of documents which previously could only be achieved by printing.

PDF

Ideal for online brochures, Adobe Acrobat **PDFs** are copies of print-based documents which can be downloaded by users. They are preferred to Word document downloads as PDFs cannot be altered. However, they require a user **plug-in** (which over 60 per cent of users have) and can produce quite high file sizes and long download times. If this is the case it can be more effective to mail a printed brochure to users instead. PDFs should also be formatted to accept US Letter and European A4 paper.

Flash

If parts of a site are designed in **Flash** then print buttons should be added, although these are often overlooked. The Flash plug-in can now print out Flash pages but this is only possible with later versions.

Backgrounds, fonts and colours

Designers can easily use printer-unfriendly layout if trying to create a unique design. White text on a black background, for example, will not show when printed, nor will non-standard fonts or poorly contrasting colours. If using Flash, large coloured backgrounds do print and can therefore waste a lot of users' printer ink.

Printing is about security. For example, short-haul airlines such as easyjet.com or buzzaway.com are ticketless but still allow users to print out sales confirmation pages so they have something physical to prove their purchase. The key to a printer-friendly site is thinking about where users would like a hard copy of any online information (particularly during the e-commerce process), even if it is not absolutely necessary.

Further information

www.adobe.com/epaper
Mistake 33 – Inappropriate use of Flash, see p. 66

The mistake   Design **Marketing** Strategy

The **browser** is the user's gateway to the Internet, with Internet Explorer dominating the browser market compared to Netscape Navigator. It goes without saying that websites need to be tested and configured to work on all versions of the major browsers. But, in addition, there are a number of marketing and design features, including **bookmarks** and 'favicons' that these browsers offer, which require simple website configuration. They not only add useful features for users, they can be used as subtle branding mechanisms.

However, few websites have considered their importance. Whilst these functions aren't going to drive huge volumes of traffic, they're perfect opportunities to get your brand right in front of customers, by integrating it with their browsers.

The solution

There are four main ways you can integrate your site into users' browsers:

Bookmarks

Bookmark lists or favourites are not a new concept so you would expect sites to have them mastered. The difficulty arises when users have a long bookmark list. Unless your site has an appropriate page-title tag, especially one which includes your company name, then your site is hard to find. Page titling also needs to be on every page, not just the home or section pages. Page titles often have long lists of keywords to aid search engineering, but these tell you nothing when you bookmark the page. So you need to choose your page titles carefully.

Default home pages

For years sites would ask users to 'make us your home page', often with lengthy text descriptions of how to do it in the tools menu of the browser – most users didn't bother. But later browsers such as Internet Explorer 5 can now do this automatically, at the click of the mouse, making it easier for your site to be the first users see every time they go online.

Favicons

Or 'favourite icons' only work with Internet Explorer 5 and later versions. They are effectively customised icons you can create, which will appear instead of the small blue and white symbol that appears to the left of web addresses in the browser address bar, or to the left of bookmarked pages. It's the ideal place to add your company logo.

Browser toolbars and accessories
Are more recent additions, that allow you to create customised toolbars that integrate into the top of browsers. Initially they have been used for news and stock tickers or for search boxes (such as with the search engine Google) but there is no reason why any site cannot create a relevant toolbar. Netscape also has a version of this called 'Sidebars'.

Further information
www.favicon.com
www.netscape.com/browsers
www.microsoft.com/ie
www.toolbar.google.com

The are three main types of user policy: terms of use, privacy/security and returns – the latter two being of the most concern to consumers. Sites do provide policies but pay little attention to them. They can be difficult to find, often hidden away in small text at the bottom of pages and are usually written by legal departments, so are long and difficult to understand. Sites also want to cover themselves for the future so the policies tend to be vague.

> In a survey of over 600 websites, 52 per cent failed to provide easily accessible information on refunds or exchanges. This is a breach of the Distance Selling Regulations that require consumer notification of cancellation and refund policies.
>
> *Source:* UK Office of Fair Trading, March 2001

The effect is that no one actually reads user policies. It is estimated that only a few per cent of all online users bother to do so. Consumers are concerned about security, privacy and returns but don't have the time to understand the details. Sites should use this as an opportunity to improve trust and consumer confidence, rather than seeing policies as distractions to the buying process.

The solution

User policies should be clearly highlighted on the home page in a place that does not require users to scroll. They are essential in the e-commerce process particularly at the start, at the point payment details are entered and for returns policies, after the sale. Policies should be written in succinct consumer-friendly English and if there is the need to create a long legal policy then create two versions of each.

Policies also need to include certain key information. 'Terms of use' can get away with more legal terminology to cover copyright, trademarks, product descriptions, links to external sites, liability and the country under which the law of the site is applicable. Privacy policies, however, create the most concern, so should include:

- What personal information is collected
- Why it is collected
- How it is used

- Whether third parties (by name or business type) use the data and details of their privacy policies
- How users can view, amend or remove information held about them
- If **cookies** are used, how and why
- How users will be informed if the policy changes (ideally by email rather than subtle changes to the wording of the website's policy page).

In all cases, users must be able to contact someone if they have a question and get a guaranteed speed of response. Returns policies should also clearly state:

- Valid return period (e.g., 30 days)
- How long it will take to recredit user accounts in the case of refunds
- If items can be returned to offline stores
- Whether delivery of returns is refunded
- Whether the company charges a 'restocking fee' for certain types of return (such as non-damaged).

Just having a range of user policies is not enough. They need to be written actively to protect consumers not just the company. If used correctly they can also be a powerful marketing tool. A good user policy therefore shouldn't be hidden. It is something to be proud of.

Further information

www.plainenglish.co.uk (campaign for jargon free communication)
www.privacy.org (useful reference site)
Mistake 13 – Ignoring the Data Protection Act, see p. 26

98 Email and Internet monitoring

The mistake

The mistake   Design   Marketing   **Strategy**

The monitoring of staff email and Internet usage is a controversial topic. Employers' powers to monitor staff came in to effect in 2000 with the UK Regulation of Investigatory Powers Act and Lawful Business Practice Legislation. Companies quote security, productivity and corporate reputation as reasons for monitoring, especially as the average worker spends two to four hours a week on personal Internet activity.

27 per cent of staff worldwide are subject to email or Internet monitoring.

Source: Privacy Foundation, July 2001

Confusion over this legislation means that companies are getting monitoring procedures wrong. For example, it is estimated that a third of companies that monitor staff keep the process hidden. Neither do companies realise that they are liable for the content of their employees' emails. As early as 1997, Norwich Union was forced to settle out of court with Western Provident Association for £450,000 due to a defamatory email sent by an employee. The effects can therefore be costly, as poor implementation opens companies to legal problems such as contravention of the Data Protection Act or calls from employees of unfair dismissal.

The solution

Monitoring software is a growth industry and is becoming less expensive. The most popular email software is MIMEsweeper, which searches and filters emails for key or obscene words, whilst a popular Internet monitor is Websense. Any company using these packages must have a formal monitoring policy, which explicitly states what is acceptable, what counts as gross misconduct and who is in charge of the monitoring process. Too often, IT departments are given responsibility for monitoring, which is questionable. Rather it should be management who make judgements on the staff being monitored. Either management should be trained to use the software, or IT only monitor an employee on the instruction of his or her manager.

Companies can officially monitor staff to:

* stop viruses
* quality control or as part of staff training
* cover key staff when on holiday
* protect corporate reputation

Above all monitoring must be justifiable. A company could fall foul of the Data Protection Act, which allows employees access to any data held about them, including that of monitoring. The Human Rights Act also protects an individual's right to privacy and implies that any monitoring must be proportional to the benefits it brings to the employer. These terms are vague and there is even confusion over the networks used. A company can monitor activity on its own **servers** but not necessarily if an employee accesses their Hotmail, for example, which is run on an Internet based server.

Privacy advocates argue that monitoring software is just an excuse for an inability to motivate and empower staff. But, if a company does want to monitor, the confusion and lack of legal precedents on which to base judgements means that policies must be made clear and monitoring must be fair and justifiable to avoid any future legal liability.

Further information

www.homeoffice.gov.uk/ripa/ripact.htm
www.privacyfoundation.org
www.mimesweeper.com
www.websense.com

99 Advertising in newsgroups and chat rooms

The mistake   Design   **Marketing**   Strategy

Newsgroups were the earliest form of online forum. There are tens of thousands of newsgroups where users can meet to discuss their particular interest or niche. Chat rooms offer a similar service. Most of the major portals such as Yahoo! or Excite have their own chat rooms and many sites, such as capitalfm.com and dobedo.com, use them to add communities to their websites. The concept is also developing into 3D virtual chat rooms and **SMS** text message chat on mobile phones.

Newsgroup advertising has traditionally been frowned upon as **spam**, often of the 'get rich quick' format. But with the growing use of **viral marketing**, mainstream brands have used postings to these forums as part of viral-marketing campaigns. By posting web addresses, thoughts and articles to often very targeted groups, the idea is that users will spread the message. Because it is a type of guerrilla marketing, it can be seen as more acceptable, particularly if targeting a younger audience who don't normally respond to traditional advertising.

But this type of advertising is deceptive and does not have the prior permission of forum members. It can easily destroy brand reputation if it is too obvious and has associations with illegal elements of forum postings such as fraudulent products and the ramping of share prices on financial discussion boards.

The solution

Some newsgroups allow advertising but you must always follow their submission rules. Often the advertiser must have a direct link to the topic of the newsgroup or there may be a separate 'product announcements' area, where multiple submissions are usually banned. A preferred alternative is explicit advertising. Many portals sell banners around forums or allow sponsorship, although there is no control over what is said in the forum, even if it reflects badly on the advertiser.

Companies have also been tempted to use customer-review sections of sites as a method of positive PR. It is easy to set up a false email account and post a glowing customer review of your product. Most such reviews are monitored and sites tend to be able to spot such deception.

The whole problem with this type of advertising is that it is hidden. There is a trend for advertisers to create campaigns or **microsites** around events, which barely mention the company involved. This subtle branding is an attempt to increase the credibility of the content. Advertorials can also take this approach. On the Internet, it can be more difficult to distinguish editorial content from advertising or sponsorship, which can lead to confusion.

There is a fine line between guerrilla marketing, clever viral campaigns and deceiving consumers. It is easier to achieve online but this doesn't make it any more acceptable. Newsgroups, chat rooms and forums are ideal for monitoring consumer groups to pick out trends and ideas, but no matter how cutting edge a viral campaign, it is not wise to use them for such deceptive advertising.

Further information

www.dejanews.com (newsgroup search engine)
Mistake 63 – Ineffective viral marketing, see p. 126

100 Colour-unfriendly pages

The Internet is primarily a visual experience, yet you don't need to look far to find sites that use unappealing colour schemes in an effort to differentiate themselves. There are only 256 'web safe' colours – and, with forty of these varying on Mac computers, this leaves just 216.

Larger corporations have well-defined brand and colour guidelines, which can be more easily translated on to the web. However, it is small to medium-sized enterprises with weaker brands, smaller design budgets and wider creative scope that tend to go off track.

The result is the use of too many colours, producing inconsistent navigation or too little contrast. This can mean the difference between purchase and site abandonment. Contrasting colours are particularly important for visually impaired or colour-blind users and poor use of colour can make page printouts difficult or unappealing to read.

The solution

Colour is very much a subjective choice on the Internet, but there are general guidelines that ensure it becomes a value-added, rather than distracting feature of your site.

Offline brand guidelines

If you have print guidelines for use with logos, direct mail, print advertising etc., these need to be adapted for your website. It's amazing how many companies pay scant attention to creating detailed, written online brand guidelines. Despite the need for a uniform brand, the web is a different medium, so print guidelines must be adapted with flexibility.

Be consistent

Any more than three or four principal colours and your site will start to lose impact, although you can extend your scheme with close matches on the colour palette. Consider the four key-colour elements of background, foreground text, navigation and links. Plus choose a scheme that is either generally lighter, generally darker or uses one concentrated 'key' colour throughout.

Site goal and meaning

Colours convey meaning. Although users' perceptions of colours are not universal, you must consider what message your site conveys. A business, e-commerce or information site will want clear, minimalist colours that don't distract. Conversely, entertainment or kids' sites will need stronger and brighter colour schemes.

Cultural differences

Don't forget that if your target audience is global, colours have different meanings in other countries. Whereas white might be associated with purity in the west (e.g., wedding sites), it represents mourning in eastern cultures.

Visual impairment

Use highly contrasting colours to reach the 5–10 per cent of male users with colour blindness, red/green blindness being the most common. A small number of companies now offer re-purposed versions of their sites for the visually impaired.

In summary, make sure your site best represents your company – ensure the colours you choose have impact, interest and identity.

Further information

www.colormatters.com (US colour information guide)
www.pantone.com
Mistake 75 – Disabled inaccessibility, see p. 150

Glossary

Bookmark
A facility available in browsers to mark a page in a website to enable easy return to it.

Broadband
A high bandwidth 'always on' Internet service that makes accessing the Internet up to ten times faster than using a standard telephone Internet connection. However, the European rollout of broadband access, particularly in Britain, has been plagued by technical problems.

Browser
Software that allows users to view and surf the Internet. The 'browser wars' have been between Microsoft's Internet Explorer and Netscape's Navigator browsers. Internet Explorer has now taken the lion's share of the browser market.

Cached page
Web pages that are stored in a PC's memory. If the same page is viewed again, a cached version can be displayed quickly from memory, rather than downloading it again from the Internet. Cached pages can cause problems when trying accurately to audit website statistics.

Click-through rate
The number of users who click on an online advertisement (e.g. a banner), expressed as a percentage of the total number of adverts displayed.

Cookie
A user profile for a particular website, which can be stored on a user's PC. They can identify a particular PC, not the individual user and their use raises questions of privacy.

CRM
Customer Relationship Management. Software and database applications to produce targeted and personalised customer relationships.

Cyber-squatter
Someone who purchases a domain name/web address (which may be a company trademark or brand name) with the intention of selling the back to the company at a profit.

dHTML
Dynamic HTML. Extension of HTML computer code that gives greater control over design and allows web pages to interact with users. Used for interactive dHTML banners, which can animate outside of the banner into the page, or capture user data.

Domain
The part of a web address that specifies a country or organisation (e.g. .com, .org). A domain name is the full web address.

Extranet
An external website only accessible to a closed user group. Often used by web design or advertising agencies to allow clients to update their website using content-management tools, or view advertising creative in a secure area.

Firewall
Security system to block unauthorised access to a computer network or website but allows authorised users and information to pass through.

Flash
Software package from the Macromedia company that can create interactive and engaging animation, navigation and web content. Requires the 'Flash plug-in', which is now automatically built into most web browsers.

Frames
A web-design technique that splits up a page into separate component parts that can be navigated independently. Used less frequently in recent years.

Hosting
Refers to who stores and maintains the server/computer where a website resides. Larger companies host their websites internally, whilst many large and small companies use one of a huge range of web-hosting companies.

HTML

Abbreviation for hypertext markup language, the standard code for designing websites. HTML emails look like a web page rather than being text only and are becoming more prevalent as more email-software packages can recognise them.

JavaScript

Programming language that makes websites more dynamic and engaging. A website using JavaScript automatically downloads a small computer program to the user's PC to allow them to view Java-based web content.

Log files

A file which records every visitor, click and interaction on a website which can be analysed by statistics packages to produce useful management information.

Megabyte

Unit of memory used to refer to the size of websites, particularly when buying server space with a web-hosting company.

Microsite

A separate and often temporary website, linked to a main website. Microsites are used for promotions, advertising campaigns and special content which merit special attention or do not fit easily into the structure of the main website.

Netiquette

Behaviour guidelines when using the Internet (e.g. asking permission from a website owner before you link to them).

Newsgroups

Internet discussion groups covering thousands of niche subject areas.

Outage

Refers to when a website fails or 'goes down' because of a server, load or technical error so that users cannot access it.

Page impressions

Total number of individual pages viewed on a website. A widely used statistic to compare the traffic and popularity of different websites.

PDF
From the Adobe company, abbreviation for portable document format. A popular document standard on the Internet, it allows documents to be scanned and viewed on any PC that has Adobe's Acrobat Reader plug-in.

Plug-in
An downloadable piece of software that allows users to view or use a proprietary applications such as document, video or audio software.

Pop-ups
Windows that appear on top of an existing website. Normally associated with pop-up advertising as well as rich-media pop-ups, such as superstitials.

Pureplay
An Internet company with no offline (e.g. high street) presence so operates solely online.

Ratecard
Standard advertising prices offered by media owners. Most clients will try and negotiate discounts off a ratecard, especially if the market is not buoyant.

Server
The computer where a website, customer or transaction data are stored.

SMS
Abbreviation for short-message service, a text-message service offered by mobile telephone networks and being increasingly used as an advertising medium.

Spam
Unsolicited, generally commercial, junk email sent to multiple and indiscriminate mailing lists.

SSL
Abbreviation for secure sockets layer, a protocol that encrypts and securely transmits data (e.g. customer credit-cards) over the Internet.

Streaming
Refers to streaming media, by which video or audio content is sent to users as a steady flow over the Internet, rather than downloading.

Superstitials
Interactive form of advertising that loads in the background of a website and then pops up. This allows it to be a larger file size than traditional banners (e.g. 100 Kilobytes) which permits greater graphics and interactivity.

Unique visitors
Measured as part of a site-statistics package, equals the number of individual users that visit a website. Differs from page impressions in that one unique visitor can view many pages when visiting a website.

Viral marketing
Form of Internet marketing whereby users pass on commercial messages to friends. If used correctly can spread to reach a wide audience at a relatively low cost.

WAP
Abbreviation for Wireless Application Protocol, which allows mobile devices to receive information or re-purposed website content. WAP has been criticised for its user interface and navigation and will be eventually superceded by 3G, which will allow more interactive, 'always on' content, such as video, to be sent wirelessly.

Useful books

D. L. Bayles, *E-Commerce Logistics and E-Commerce Fulfillment*, Prentice-Hall, 2001.

K. Couplan, *Web Works Navigation*, Rockport Publishing, 2000.

R. Danielson, *Homepage and Splashpage*, Rockport Publishers, 2000.

J. Eglash, *How to Write a .com Business Plan*, McGraw-Hill, 2000.

J. Griffin & M.W. Lowenstein, *Customer Winback*, Jossey Bass Wiley, 2001.

S. Hamlin, *Effective Web Animation*, Addison Wesley, 1999.

A. J. Kim, *Community Building on the Web*, Peachpit Press, 2000.

M. Lindstrom & T. F. Andersen, *Brand Building on the Internet*, Kogan Page, 2000.

F. Marckini, *Search Engine Positioning*, Wordware Publishing, 2001.

S. McLure et al, *Hacking Exposed*, Osborne McGraw-Hill, 2001.

R. Nakano, *Web Content Management*, Addison Wesley, 2001.

J. Nielsen & M.Tahir, *Homepage Usability*, New Riders Publishing, 2001.

M. Paciello, *Web Accessibility for People with Disabilities*, R&D Books, 2000.

W. Sonnereich & T. Macinta, *Web Developer .com Guide to Search Engines*, John Wiley & Sons, 1998.

J. Sterne, *Email Marketing*, John Wiley & Sons, 2000.

A. Tiwana, *The Essential Guide to Knowledge Management: E-Business and CRM Applications*, Prentice Hall, 2000.